The Strength and Genius of Booker T. Washington

∽

William J. Federer

Richard M. Federer

Copyright 8/02/23 William J. Federer, Richard M. Federer.
All rights reserved.

Conditions of Use: Permission granted to duplicate less than 5,000 words provided acknowledgment is given.

The Strength and Genius of Booker T. Washington
by William J. Federer, Richard M. Federer

Library of Congress
BIOGRAPHY / UNITED STATES HISTORY
ISBN-13: ISBN: 978-1-7369590-3-9

Dedicated to Bishop Robert E. Smith, Sr.
Overcomers, Total Outreach for Christ Ministries
Little Rock, Arkansas

Cover design:
Dustin Myers, LongitudeDesign.com
(417) 986-2336 dustin@longitudebranding.com

Cover image credits: Public Domain; Booker T. Washington; Harris & Ewing; January 1, 1905; http://hdl.loc.gov/loc.pnp/hec.16114 ; U.S. Library of Congress's Prints and Photographs division under the digital ID ppmsca.23961 ; https://en.wikipedia.org/wiki/File:Booker_T_Washington_retouched_flattened-crop.jpg

For a limited time, you may receive this title as an **ebook**. Email richmfederer@gmail.com with subject line "Booker." A pdf file will be sent by reply email.

Amerisearch, Inc.
1-888-USA-WORD, 314-346-7740
richmfederer@gmail.com
www.AmericanMinute.com

*If you want to lift yourself up,
lift up someone else.*
– Booker T. Washington

*The happiest people are those who do
the most for others. The most miserable
are those who do the least.*
– Booker T. Washington

We must learn to incorporate God's laws into our thoughts and words and acts. Frequent reference is made in the Bible to the freedom that comes from being a Christian.
– Booker T. Washington

Remember that the only way to show ourselves superior to others is to excel them in kindlier impulses and more generous deeds.
.– Booker T. Washington

I will permit no man to narrow and degrade my soul by making me hate him.
– Booker T. Washington

CONTENTS

Foreword 7
1. Early Years 9
2. Hampton Institute 25
3. Wayland Baptist Seminary 37
4. Founding Tuskegee Institute 39
5. Need For Economic Success 53
6. Washington's Wisdom 59
7. Frederick Douglass & William Lloyd Garrison. 63
8. Love Thy Neighbor 67
9. Christian Charity & Donors to Tuskegee 73
10. Views on the Bible 79
11. Atlanta Exposition 83
12. George Washington Carver 91
13. Christianity at Tuskegee 105
14. President William McKinley's Visit 109
15. Harvard Honorary Doctorate & Recognition... 115
16. Advisor to Presidents 121
17. Rising Above Critics 135
18. Martin Luther King, Jr. 147
19. Death and Legacy 155
20. Final Thoughts 157

*The men doing the vital things of life
are those who read the Bible ...
and not ashamed to let the world know it.*
– Booker T. Washington

FOREWORD

Booker T. Washington was born into slavery, not knowing who his father was, yet he ended up befriending the world's most powerful business leaders and advising Presidents. From teaching himself to read he went on to be president of a university. From working in a salt furnace and coal mine he founded a national business league. From obscurity he rose to become one of the most renown orators in the nation.

He faced prejudice and discrimination yet did not become bitter or yield to victimhood. He experienced personal tragedy with the death of his first wife followed five years later by the death of his second, yet he did not succumb to depression. He was criticized in the press by detractors and communist agitators but responded with dignity.

He wrote books, had schools named after him, as well as monuments, a state park, a bridge, a ship, a plane, and a mountain. His birthplace in Virginia was declared a National Memorial and his bust placed in the Hall of Fame in New York. His image was on U.S. Postage stamps and a 50-cent coin. Historians refer to 1880-1915 as the Age of Booker T. Washington.

His timeless wisdom inspired millions, and after reading this book, hopefully inspire you!

1. EARLY YEARS

Booker T. Washington was one of the most significant figures in post Reconstruction America. His life's work advanced the educational and economic condition of blacks in the United States. He authored 14 books, such as *Up From Slavery*, which continue to be widely read today.

His mother, Jane, was a cook on the James Burroughs plantation near Hale's Ford in Franklin County, Virginia. On April 5, 1856, he was born in a slave hut, though no record exists. He celebrated his birthday on Easter. His worth was listed on Burroughs' property inventory as $400.

In *The Story of My Life & Work*, 1901, Washington wrote:

> I was asked not long ago to tell something about the sports and pastimes that I engaged in during my youth. Until that question was asked it had never occurred to me that there was no period of my life that was devoted to play.
>
> From the time that I can remember anything, almost every day of my life has been occupied in some kind of labor ... During the period that I spent in slavery I was not large enough to be of much service, still I was occupied most of the time in cleaning the yards, carrying water to the men in the fields,

or going to the mill, to which I used to take the corn, once a week, to be ground.

Booker was five years old in 1861 when the Civil War began. Democrat Senator Jefferson Davis from Mississippi became the President of the Confederacy. He stated:

> African slavery, as it exists in the United States, is a moral, a social, and a political blessing.

Abraham Lincoln, a Republican, stated in Springfield, Illinois, June 26, 1857:

> Two weeks ago Judge Douglas spoke here on the ... Dred Scott decision ... He finds the Republicans insisting that the Declaration of Independence includes ALL men, black as well as white ... He boldly denies that it includes Negroes ... I protest against that ...
>
> Chief Justice Taney, in his opinion in the Dred Scott case, admits that the language of the Declaration is broad enough to include the whole human family, but he and Judge Douglas argue that the authors of that instrument did not intend to include Negroes ...
>
> I think the authors of that noble instrument intended to include all men ... Dred Scott, his wife and two daughters were all involved in the suit ... Judge Douglas is delighted to have them decided to be slaves ...
>
> How differently the respective courses of the Democratic and Republican parties ...

> Republicans inculcate ... that the Negro is a man; that his bondage is cruelly wrong ...
>
> Democrats deny his manhood; deny, or dwarf to insignificance, the wrong of his bondage; so far as possible, crush all sympathy for him, and cultivate and excite hatred and disgust against him.

Lincoln became the 16th President in 1861. He addressed the Indiana Regiment, March 17, 1865:

> Whenever I hear anyone arguing for slavery, I feel a strong impulse to see it tried on him personally.

Lincoln proclaimed in his Gettysburg Address, November 19, 1863:

> Four score and seven years ago our fathers brought forth on this continent, a new nation, conceived in Liberty, and dedicated to the proposition that all men are created equal. Now we are engaged in a great civil war, testing whether that nation, or any nation so conceived and so dedicated, can long endure.

General Ulysses S. Grant, who later was a Republican President, recalled in 1878 his thoughts when he heard the Civil War had started:

> As soon as slavery fired upon the flag it was felt, we all felt ... that slavery must be destroyed. We felt that it was a stain to the Union that men should be bought and sold like cattle.

Booker wrote in *The Story of My Life and Work*, 1901:

> So far as I can now recall, the first

knowledge that I got of the fact that we were slaves, and that freedom of the slaves was being discussed, was early one morning before day, when I was awakened by my mother kneeling over her children and fervently praying that Lincoln and his armies might be successful, and that one day she and her children might be free.

A major turning point in the Civil War was the Battle of Antietam, September 17, 1862, the bloodiest day of fighting in American history with over 23,000 casualties. The North was able to replace its fallen ranks by drafting European immigrants from crowded northern cities, but the South was agricultural and did not have the population base from which to draw new recruits. It was a war of attrition.

Lincoln, the first Republican President, met with his cabinet to draft the Emancipation Proclamation. Secretary of the Treasury Salmon Portland Chase recorded Lincoln declaring:

> The time for the annunciation of the emancipation policy can no longer be delayed. Public sentiment will sustain it, many of my warmest friends and supporters demand it, and I have promised God that I will do it.

When asked what he meant, Lincoln replied:

> I made a solemn vow before God, that if General Lee were driven back from Pennsylvania, I would crown the result by the declaration of freedom to the slaves.

The Emancipation Proclamation stated:

> I, Abraham Lincoln, President of the United States, by virtue of the power in me vested as Commander-in-Chief ... do, on the first day of January, in the year of our Lord one thousand eight hundred and sixty-three ... publicly proclaim ... that ... persons held as slaves ... are, and henceforward shall be, free ...
>
> And I hereby enjoin upon the people so declared to be free to abstain from all violence ... and ... labor faithfully for reasonable wages ...
>
> And upon this act ... I invoke ... the gracious favor of Almighty God.

Booker T. Washington was nine years old when the war ended. He remembered:

> There was more singing in the slave quarters than usual ... Most of the verses of the plantation songs had some reference to freedom ... Some man who seemed to be a stranger (a United States officer, I presume) made a little speech and then read a rather long paper — the Emancipation Proclamation ...
>
> After the reading we were told that we were all free and could go when and where we pleased.
>
> My mother, who was standing by my side, leaned over and kissed her children, while tears of joy ran down her cheeks. She explained to us what it all meant, that this was the day for which she had been so long praying but fearing that she would never live to see.

Lincoln rushed to push through Congress the 13th Amendment to abolish slavery before the war ended, as his Emancipation Proclamation was issued using Presidential war powers which would end once the war ended. He also feared that after the war, the southern states readmitted to the Union may block the Amendment's ratification and re-institute a form of slavery.

The 13th Amendment was passed by the U.S. Senate on April 8, 1864. All 30 Republican Senators voted in favor of it, joined by 4 Democrats.

The U.S. House passed the 13th Amendment on January 31, 1865. All 86 Republicans voted in favor of it, joined by 15 Democrats, 14 Unconditional Unionists, and 4 Union men. Voting against the 13th Amendment were 50 Democrat Congressmen, joined by 6 Union men.

Though not necessary, Lincoln added his signature to the 13th Amendment after the words "Approved February 1, 1865."

Lincoln said in his Second Annual Message, December 1, 1862:

> In giving freedom to the slave, we assure freedom to the free ... We shall nobly save — or meanly lose — the last, best hope of earth. Other means may succeed; this could not fail.
>
> The way is plain ... a way which if followed the world will forever applaud and God must forever bless.

Nearly a half-million died fighting in the Civil War which freed four million slaves.

In Charleston, South Carolina, a mass grave was uncovered of 257 Union soldiers who had died in a prison camp. On May 1, 1865, former slaves organized a parade, led by 2,800 singing black children, in which they prayed, read Bible verses, sang spirituals, and reburied the soldiers with honor as an act of gratefulness for their ultimate sacrifice which gave them freedom.

News of freedom from slavery finally reached Galveston, Texas, June 19, 1865, resulting in that date being celebrated annually as "Juneteenth."

Booker T. Washington wrote in *The Story of My Life & Work*:

> The wild rejoicing on the part of the emancipated colored people lasted but for a brief period, for I noticed that by the time they returned to their cabins there was a change in their feelings.
>
> The great responsibility of being free, of having charge of themselves, of having to think and plan for themselves and their children, seemed to take possession of them. It was very much like suddenly turning a youth of ten or twelve years out into the world to provide for himself.
>
> In a few hours ... great questions ... had been thrown upon these people to be solved. These were the questions of a home, a living, the rearing of children, education, citizenship, and the establishment and support of churches.
>
> Was it any wonder that within a few hours the wild rejoicing ceased

and a feeling of deep gloom seemed to pervade the slave quarters? To some it seemed that, now that they were in actual possession of it, freedom was a more serious thing than they had expected to find it.

The 14th Amendment to force Southern States to give rights to freed slaves was passed in the U.S. House on May 10, 1866, and in the U.S. Senate on June 8, 1866. One hundred percent of Democrats voted against it. It was adopted by the States on July 28, 1868.

Republican Congressman John Farnsworth of Illinois explained, March 31, 1871:

> The reason for the adoption (of the 14th Amendment) ... was because of ... discriminating ... legislation of those States ... by which they were punishing one class of men under different laws from another class."

In *Up From Slavery: An Autobiography*, 1904, Booker T. Washington wrote of his mother, Jane, and his stepfather, Washington Ferguson:

> My mother's husband, who was the stepfather of my brother John and myself, did not belong to the same owners as did my mother. In fact, he seldom came to our plantation. I remember seeing him there perhaps once a year, that being about Christmas time.
>
> In some way, during the war, by running away and following the Federal soldiers, it seems, he found his way into the new state of West Virginia. As soon

as freedom was declared, he sent for my mother to come to the Kanawha Valley, in West Virginia.

At that time a journey from Virginia over the mountains to West Virginia was rather a tedious and in some cases a painful undertaking. What little clothing and few household goods we had were placed in a cart, but the children walked the greater portion of the distance, which was several hundred miles.

Washington wrote:

We began life in West Virginia in a little shanty and lived in it for several years. My step-father soon obtained work for my brother John and myself in the salt furnaces and coal mines, and we worked alternately in them until about the year 1871.

Soon after we reached West Virginia a schoolteacher, Mr. William Davis, came into the community, and the colored people induced him to open a school. My step-father was not able to spare me from work so that I could attend this school when it was first opened, and this proved a sore disappointment to me.

I remember that soon after going to Malden, West Virginia, I saw a young colored man among a large number of colored people, reading a newspaper, and this fired my ambition to learn to read as nothing had done before. I said to myself, if I could ever reach the point where I could read as this man was doing, the acme of my ambition would be reached ...

In all my efforts to learn to read, my mother shared fully my ambition and sympathized with me and aided me in every way she could. If I have done anything in life worth attention, I feel sure that I inherited the disposition from my mother ...

Although I could not attend the school, I remember that, in some way, my mother secured a book for me, and although she could not read herself, she tried in every way possible to help me to do so ...

Every barrel of salt that was packed in the mines was marked, and by watching the letters that were put on the salt barrels I soon learned to read.

As time went on, after considerable persuasion on my part, my step-father consented to permit me to attend the public school half of the day, provided I would get up very early in the morning and perform as much work as possible before school time. This permission brought me great joy. By four o'clock in the morning I was up and at my work, which continued until nearly nine o'clock. The first day I entered school, it seems to me, was the happiest day that I have ever known.

The first embarrassment I experienced at school was in the matter of finding a name for myself. I had always been called "Booker," and had not known that one had use for more than one name. Some of the slaves took the surnames of their owners, but after freedom there was a prejudice against doing this, and a large part of the colored people gave themselves new names.

When the teacher called the roll, I noticed that he called each pupil by two names, that is a given name and a surname. When he came to me, he asked for my full name, and I told him to put me down as "Booker Washington," and that name I have borne ever since. It is not every schoolboy who has the privilege of choosing his own name.

He continued:

My step-father seemed to be over careful that I should continue my work in the salt furnace until nine o'clock each day. This practice made me late at school, and often caused me to miss my lessons. To overcome this, I resorted to a practice of which I am not now very proud, and it is one of the few things I did as a child of which I am now ashamed.

There was a large clock in the salt furnace that kept the time for hundreds of workmen connected with the salt furnace and coal mine.

But, as I found myself continually late at school, and after missing some of my lessons, I yielded to the temptation to move forward the hands on the dial of the clock so as to give enough time to permit me to get to school in time.

This went on for several days, until the manager found the time so unreliable that the clock was locked up in a case.

Washington continued:

It was in Malden that I first found out what a Sunday school meant. I remember that I was playing marbles one Sunday morning in the road with a number of other boys, and an old colored man passed by on his way to Sunday school. He spoke a little harshly to us about playing marbles on Sunday, and asked why we did not go to Sunday school. He explained in a few broken though plain words what a Sunday school meant and what benefit we would get from it by going.

His words impressed me so that I put away my marbles and followed him to Sunday school, and thereafter was in regular attendance ... Some years afterwards, I became one of the teachers in this Sunday school and finally became its superintendent.

He wrote in *Story of My Life & Work*, 1901:

No matter how dark the days or how discouraging the circumstances, there was never a time in my youth when the firm resolution to secure an education, at any cost, did not constantly remain with me.

Next came the unpleasant coal mine experience. My step-father was not able, however, to permit me to continue in school long, even for a half day at the time. I was soon taken out of school and put to work in the coal mine.

As a child I recall now the fright which, going a long distance under the mountain into a dark and damp coal mine, gave me. It seemed to me that the distance from the opening of the mine to the place where I had to work was at least a mile and a half.

Although I had to leave school, I did not give up my search for knowledge. I took my book into the coal mine, and during the spare minutes I tried to read by the light of the little lamp which hung on my cap.

Not long after I began to work in the mines, my mother hired someone to teach me at night, but often, after walking a considerable distance for a night's lesson, I found that my teacher knew but little more than I did. This, however, was not the case with Mr. William Davis, my first teacher.

Booker then worked for the Ruffners, a strict Presbyterian family that ran a successful salt mining and production business in town.

After working in the coal mine for some time, my mother secured a position for me as house boy in the family of General Lewis Ruffner. I went to live with this family with a good many fears and doubts. General Ruffner's wife, Mrs. Viola Ruffner, had the reputation of being very strict and hard to please, and most of the boys who had been employed by her had remained only a short time with her ...

She paid me, or rather my step-father, six dollars per month and board for my work. When I could not get the opportunity to attend school in the afternoon, I resorted to my old habit of having someone teach me at night, although I had to walk a good distance after my work was done in order to do this.

A Unionist, General Lewis Ruffner's elder brother, Rev. Henry Ruffner, was President of Washington College. He caused a stir prior to the Civil War by publishing an anti-slavery pamphlet.

Lewis Ruffner was a leader of an emancipation society and was one of the founders of the free State of West Virginia, which, during the Civil War, had broken away from the Confederate State of Virginia.

In 1868, Lewis Ruffner was attacked by a mob of about 100 for hiring black men to work in his salt manufacturing business. He suffered injuries from which he never fully recovered.

Mrs. Viola Ruffner, who had been a Vermont schoolteacher, worked with Booker on his education. He credited this time as training him in the value of a dollar and in the Puritan work ethic of cleanliness, promptness, honesty, and thrift. He described Mrs. Viola Ruffner as "one of the best friends I ever had."

Lewis and Viola were faithful benefactors to Washington the rest of their lives. Descendants of both the Washington family and the Ruffner family are still friends to this day and contribute together to causes for the growth of society.

Washington continued:

> While living with Mrs. Ruffner I got some very valuable experience in another direction, that of marketing and selling vegetables. Mrs. Ruffner was very fond of raising grapes and vegetables, and, although I was quite a boy, she entrusted me with the responsibility of selling a large portion of these products. I became very fond of this work. I remember that I used to go to the houses of the miners and prevail upon them to buy these things.
>
> I think at first Mrs. Ruffner doubted whether or not I would be honest in these transactions, but as time went on and she found the cash from these sales constantly increasing her confidence grew in me, and before I left her service, she willingly trusted me with anything in her possession. I always made it a special point to return to her at the end of each campaign as a salesman every cent that I had received and to let her see how many vegetables or how much fruit was brought back unsold.
>
> At one time I remember that, when I passed by an acquaintance of mine when I had a large basket of peaches for sale, he took the liberty of walking up to me and taking one of the ripest and most tempting peaches.

Although he was a man and I was but a boy, I gave him to understand in the most forceful manner that I would not permit it. He seemed greatly surprised that I would not let him take one peach. He tried to explain to me that no one would miss it and that I would be none the worse off for his taking it.

When he could not bring me to his way of thinking he tried to frighten me by force into yielding, but I had my way, and I am sure that this man respected me all the more for being honest with other people's property. I told him that if the peaches were mine, I would gladly let him have one; but under no circumstances could I consent to let him take without a protest that which was entrusted to me by others.

It happened very often that as I would pass through the streets with a large basket of grapes or other fruit, many of the larger boys tried by begging and then by force to dispossess me of a portion of what had been given me to sell, but I think there was no instance when I yielded.

From my earliest childhood I have always had it implanted in me that it never pays to be dishonest, and that reward, at some time, in some manner, for the performance of conscientious duty, will always come, and in this I have never been disappointed.

2. HAMPTON INSTITUTE

In 1872, at the age of 16, Booker T. Washington left Malden and traversed nearly 500 miles to attend the Hampton Institute in Virginia. He wrote in *Story of My Life & Work*, 1901:

> After my mother and brother John had secured me a few extra garments, with what I could provide for myself, I started for Hampton, about the first of October, 1872. How long I was on this journey I have at this time no very definite idea.
>
> Part of the way I went by railroad, part in a stage, and part on foot. I remember that when I got as far as Richmond, Virginia, I was completely out of money, and knew not a single person in the city. Besides, I had never been in a city before. I think it was about nine o'clock at night that I reached Richmond. I was hungry, tired and dirty, and had nowhere to go. I wandered about the streets until about midnight, when I felt completely exhausted.
>
> By chance I came to a street that had a plank sidewalk, and I crept under this sidewalk and spent the night. The next morning, I felt very much rested, but was still quite hungry, as it had been some time since I had a good meal.

When I awoke, I noticed some ships not far from where I had spent the night.

I went to one of these vessels and asked the captain to permit me to work for him, so that I could earn some money to get some food. The captain very kindly gave me work, which was that of helping to unload pig iron from the vessel. In my rather weak and hungry condition I found this hard work, but I stuck to it, and was given enough money to buy a little food.

My work seemed to have pleased the master of the vessel so much that he furnished me with work for several days, but I continued to sleep under the sidewalk each night, for I was anxious to save enough money to pay my passage to Hampton.

After working on this vessel for some days, I started again for Hampton, and arrived there in a day or two, with a surplus of fifty cents in my pocket. I did not let anyone know how forlorn my condition was. I feared that if I did, I would be rejected as one that was altogether too unpromising.

The first person I saw after reaching the Hampton Institute was Miss Mary F. Mackie, the Lady Principal. After she had asked me many searching questions, with a good deal of doubt and hesitation in her manner, I was assigned to a room.

She remarked at the same time that it

would be decided later whether I could be admitted as a student. I shall not soon forget the impression that the sight of a good, clean, comfortable room and bed made upon me, for I had not slept in a bed since I left my home in West Virginia.

Within a few hours I presented myself again before Miss Mackie to hear my fate, but she still seemed to be undecided. Instead of telling me whether or not I could remain, I remember, she showed me a large recitation room and told me to sweep it.

I felt at once that the sweeping of that room would decide my case. I knew I could sweep, for Mrs. Ruffner had taught me that art well. I think that I must have swept that room over as many as three times and dusted it the same number of times.

After a while Miss Mackie came into the room and rubbed her handkerchief over the tables and benches to see if I had left any dust, but not a particle could she find. She remarked with a smile, "I guess we will try you as a student." At that moment I think I was the happiest individual that ever entered the Hampton Institute ...

After I had succeeded in passing my "sweeping examination," I was assigned by Miss Mackie to the position of assistant janitor. This position, with the exception of working on the farm for a while, I held during the time I was a student at Hampton. I took care of four or five classrooms; that is, I swept and dusted them and built the fires when needed. A great portion of the time I had to rise at four o'clock in the morning in order to do my work and find time to prepare my lessons ...

While at Hampton my best friends did not know how badly off I was for clothing during a large part of the time, but I did not fret about that. I always had the feeling that if I could get knowledge in my head, the matter of clothing would take care of itself afterwards. At one time I was reduced to a single ragged pair of cheap socks. These socks I had to wash over night and put them on the next morning ...

(A) valuable lesson I learned at the Hampton Institute was the use of the bath. I learned there for the first time some of its value, not only in keeping the body healthy, but in inspiring self-respect and promoting virtue.

In all my travels in the South and elsewhere, since leaving Hampton, I have always in some way sought my daily bath. To get it sometimes when I have been the guest of my own people in a single-roomed cabin has not always been easy to do, except by slipping away to some stream in the woods.

I have always tried to teach my people that some provision for bathing should be a part of every house.

The Hampton Institute was founded by General Samuel Chapman Armstrong. Washington wrote:

> After I had been at the Hampton Institute a day or two, I saw General Armstrong, the Principal, and he made the impression upon me of being the most perfect specimen of man, physically, mentally and spiritually, that I had ever seen; and I have never had occasion to change my first impression.
>
> In fact, as the years went by and as I came to know him better, the feeling grew. I have never seen a man in whom I had such confidence. It never occurred to me that it was possible for him to fail in anything that he undertook to accomplish.
>
> I have sometimes thought that the best part of my education at Hampton was obtained by being permitted to look upon General Armstrong day by day. He was a man who could not endure for a minute hypocrisy or want of truth in anyone. This moral lesson he impressed upon everyone who came in contact with him.

General Armstrong was born on the Pacific Island of Maui in 1839 to Protestant missionaries Rev. Richard and Clarissa Chapman Armstrong.

Rev. Armstrong was Senior Pastor of the famous Kawaiaha'o Church in Honolulu, which was the national church of the Kingdom of Hawaii. King Kamehameha III appointed him President of Hawaii's Board of Education.

Young Samuel Armstrong sailed to Massachusetts and attended Williams College in Williamstown. A classmate of his was James Garfield, the future 20th U.S. President. After graduation in 1862, both Armstrong and Garfield joined the U.S. Army.

Armstrong was strongly anti-slavery and wrote that the war should not end until "every slave ... can call himself his own, and his wife and children his own." Promoted to a captain in the 125th New York Infantry, he was captured at Harper's Ferry, was exchanged, and returned back to duty.

He served in the 3rd Division of I Corps under General Alexander Hays and fought at the Battle of Gettysburg, defending Cemetery Ridge against Pickett's Charge, July 3, 1863. He was promoted to lieutenant colonel of the newly formed United States Colored Troops, assigned as executive officer of the 9th USCT.

As pre-war slave codes in Democrat states forbade teaching slaves to read or write, Armstrong established a school to educate black troops at Camp Stanton near Benedict, Maryland.

Armstrong then commanded the 8th USCT in the fierce battles of Deep Bottom and Fussell's Mill. They fought in the siege of Petersburg, being the first troops to enter the city on April 3, 1865, receiving "a most cheering and hearty welcome from the colored inhabitants of the city, whom their presence had made free."

Armstrong's unit of U.S. Colored Troops fought in the Appomattox Campaign, and was later stationed at Ringgold Barracks near Rio

Grande City, Texas.

On January 13, 1866, President Andrew Johnson nominated Armstrong as a brevet brigadier general of volunteers, and the US Senate confirmed his new commission. After the Civil War, 1866-1868, Armstrong worked with the Bureau of Refugees, Freedmen, and Abandoned Land (Freedmen's Bureau).

He wanted to help newly freed blacks receive the benefit of an education so they could compete and succeed. He founded the Hampton Institute with the help of the American Missionary Association (AMA), a Protestant Christian abolitionist group. He laid out the vision of the moral power of literacy and labor:

> The solution lay in a Hampton-styled education, an education that combined cultural uplift with moral and manual training ... an education that encompassed the head, the heart, and the hands.

Students studied English, arithmetic, geography, basic science, and history. As students had little money, and the school had no endowment, students helped out by working in the school's shops or on the school farm. Booker's job as a janitor allowed him to interact with the school staff and gain valuable insights into the practical side of running a college.

Approximately 84 percent of the first 723 graduates became teachers, with others becoming doctors, lawyers, ministers, and politicians.

Washington considered General Armstrong

"more than a father," describing him as "the noblest, rarest human being that it has ever been my privilege to meet" and "the most perfect specimen of a man, physically, mentally, and spiritually, the most Christ-like."

Washington added:

> I have spoken of my admiration for General Armstrong, and yet he was but a type of that Christ-like body of men and women who went into the Negro schools at the close of the war by the hundreds to assist in lifting up my race.
>
> The history of the world fails to show a higher, purer, and more unselfish class of men and women than those who found their way into those Negro schools.

Hampton Institute was a boarding school, with students learning housekeeping, personal hygiene, etiquette and Christian morality. Washington wrote in *The Story of My Life & Work*:

> While taking the regular literary and industrial courses at Hampton, next to my regular studies I was most fond of the debating societies, of which there were two or three. The first subject that I debated in public was whether or not the execution of Maj. Andre was justifiable. (*Andre was a captured British spy during the Revolutionary War.)
>
> After I had been at Hampton a few months I helped to organize the "After Supper Club." I noticed that the students usually had about twenty minutes after

tea when no special duty called them; so about twenty-five of us agreed to come together each evening and spend those twenty minutes in the discussion of some important subject.

These meetings were a constant source of delight and were most valuable in preparing us for public speaking.

Washington wrote in *Up From Slavery*, 1901:

Perhaps the most valuable thing that I got out of my second year at the Hampton Institute was an understanding of the use and value of the Bible.

Miss Nathalie Lord, one of the teachers, from Portland, Maine, taught me how to use and love the Bible ... I learned to love to read the Bible, not only for the spiritual help which it gives, but on account of it as literature.

The lessons taught me in this respect took such a hold upon me that at the present time, when I am at home, no matter how busy I am, I always make it a rule to read a chapter or a portion of a chapter in the morning, before beginning the work of the day.

Whatever ability I may have as a public speaker I owe in a measure to Miss Lord.

He wrote in *The Story of My Life and Work* (1901):

Aside from Gen. Armstrong, Gen. Marshall and Miss Mackie, the persons who made the deepest impression upon me at Hampton were Miss Nathalie Lord and Miss Elizabeth Brewer, two teachers from New England.

> I am especially indebted to these two for being helped in my spiritual life and led to love and understand the Bible. Largely by reason of their teaching, I find that a day rarely, if ever, passes when I am at home, that I do not read the Bible.

Miss Natalie Lord wrote in an article for the Hampton Institution publication, *The Southern Workman* (May 1902):

> Booker, as we always called him ... I was much interested in him from the first. His quiet, unassuming manner, his earnestness of purpose and faithfulness greatly impressed me. I saw in him one whom you could completely trust. He was diligent in his business ... and yet unselfish in his thought for others.

Washington wrote in *The Story of My Life & Work*:

> After I had remained at Hampton for two years, I went back to West Virginia to spend my four months of vacation.
>
> Soon after my return to Malden my mother, who was never strong, died. I do not remember how old I was at this time, but I do remember that it was during my vacation from Hampton.
>
> I had been without work for some time, and had been off several miles looking for work. On returning home at night I was very tired, and stopped in the

boiler-room of one of the engines used to pump salt water into the salt furnace near my home. I was so tired that I soon fell asleep. About two or three o'clock in the morning, someone, my brother John, I think, found me and told me that our mother was dead.

It has always been a source of indescribable pain to me that I was not present when she passed away, but the lessons of truth, honor and thrift which she implanted in me while she lived have remained with me, and I consider them among my most precious possessions. She seemed never to tire of planning ways for me and the other children to get an education and to make true men and women of us, although she herself was without education.

This was the severest trial I had ever experienced, because she always sympathized with me deeply in every effort that I made to get on in the world.

He added:

My sister Amanda was too young to know how to take care of the house, and my step-father was too poor to hire anyone. Sometimes we had food cooked for our meals and sometimes we did not. During the whole of the summer, after the death of my mother, I do not think there was a time when the whole family sat down to a meal together.

By working for Mrs. Ruffner and others, and by the aid of my brother

John, I obtained money enough to return to Hampton in the fall, and graduated in the regular course in the summer of 1875.

Another famous graduate of the Hampton Institute was Thomas Calhoun Walker. He went on to study law under former Confederate General William Booth Taliaferro. T.C. Walker passed the Virginia Bar in 1887, and tirelessly defended African-Americans from unjust arrest. He was elected to the Gloucester County Board of Supervisors in 1891 and appointed by President William McKinley as Virginia's first black Collector of Customs in 1896.

In 1934, T.C. Walker was named by President Franklin Roosevelt as advisor of Negro Affairs for the Virginia Emergency Relief Administration, earning him the nickname "Black Governor of Virginia." He was superintendent of Gloucester County Negro Schools and built African-American schools in eastern Virginia.

Another Hampton Institute graduate was James Apostle Fields. He earned a law degree from Howard University, served two terms in the Virginia General Assembly, and served as a school superintendent. Fields' home became the first African-American hospital in the lower Virginia Peninsula.

3. WAYLAND BAPTIST SEMINARY

Booker T. Washington graduated from the Hampton Institute in 1875 at the age of 20. He wrote:

> After finishing the course at Hampton, I went to Saratoga Springs, in New York, and was a waiter during the summer at the United States Hotel, the same hotel at which I have several times since been a guest upon the invitation of friends.

He then moved back to Malden where he worked in the salt industry, saving money to help pay the tuition for his brother, John, and an adopted brother, James, to attend the Hampton Institute.

He began a night school, educating some 80 students and became well-respected in the community. He also taught a Sunday School class at the African Zion Baptist Church.

At the age of the age of 22, he had earned enough money to travel to Washington, D.C., where he attended Wayland Baptist Seminary, founded by the American Baptist Home Mission Society. He wrote:

> In 1878, I went to Wayland Seminary, in Washington, and spent a year in study there. Rev. G.M.P. King, D.D., was

President of the Wayland Seminary while I was a student there.

> Notwithstanding I was there but a short time, the high Christian character of Dr. King made a lasting impression upon me. The deep religious spirit which pervaded the atmosphere at Wayland made an impression upon me which I trust will always remain.

He continued:

> Soon after my year at Wayland was completed, I was invited by a committee of gentlemen in Charleston, West Virginia, to stump the state of West Virginia in the interest of having the capital of the state moved from Wheeling, West Virginia, to Charleston ...
>
> After about three months of campaigning the voters declared in favor of Charleston as the permanent capital, by a large majority. I ... had the satisfaction of feeling that my efforts counted for something in winning success for Charleston, which is only five miles from my old home, Malden.

4. FOUNDING TUSKEGEE INSTITUTE

In 1879, Booker was called back to the Hampton Institute where he was hired as a teacher. He also served as a dorm father to 50 native American students.

Two years later, in 1881, the State of Alabama voted to establish an industrial institute for blacks similar to the Hampton Institute. General Armstrong was asked who he would recommend be principal of the new school. He confidently recommended Booker T. Washington as the most qualified for the position.

At the age of 25, Washington traveled to Alabama and founded Tuskegee Normal and Industrial Institute on July 4, 1881, with 37 students, meeting in the Butler Chapel African Methodist Episcopal Zion Church. The next year, Washington purchased land where students made bricks and built the first buildings. During his tenure, the school grew to over 2,000 students and a faculty of 200 teaching 40 trades. He described the early years:

> The coming of Christmas, that first year of our residence in Alabama, gave us an opportunity to get a farther insight into the real life of the people.
>
> The first thing that reminded us that Christmas had arrived was the "foreday"

visits of scores of children rapping at our doors, asking for "Chris'mus gifts! Chris'mus gifts!" Between the hours of two o'clock and five o'clock in the morning I presume that we must have had a half-hundred such calls.

This custom prevails throughout this portion of the South to-day. During the days of slavery, it was a custom quite generally observed throughout all the Southern states to give the colored people a week of holiday at Christmas.

In 1882, Washington married his sweetheart from Malden, Fannie Norton Smith. She was one of his students when he taught there and he helped her get accepted at the Hampton Institute. She gave birth to their daughter, Portia, in 1883.

Washington raised funds and the school soon purchased a farm. Students worked on campus instead of paying tuition. This is a financial model used today in schools, such as College of the Ozarks. This way students not only learned academics, but also trade skills, such as how to grow their own crops and raise livestock.

In 1884, tragedy struck. Fannie died, possibly from injuries from falling off a wagon. He wrote:

> During the summer of 1882, at the end of our first year's work, I was married to Miss Fannie N. Smith, of Malden, West Virginia, and we began housekeeping in Tuskegee early in the fall. This made a home for our teachers, who had now been increased to four in number. My wife was also a graduate

of the Hampton Institute. After earnest and constant work in the interest of the school, together with her housekeeping duties, she passed away in May, 1884. One child, Portia M. Washington, was born during our marriage.

From the first, my wife most earnestly devoted her thought and time to the work of the school, and was completely one with me in every interest and ambition. She died, however, before she had an opportunity of seeing what the school was destined to be.

The following account of her death is taken from the *Alumni Journal*, published at the time at Hampton:

"The numerous friends of Mr. B.T. Washington will be pained to learn of the death of his beloved wife, Mrs. Fannie (Smith) Washington, class of '82, which occurred at Tuskegee, Alabama, Sunday, May 4th.

"Her death is indeed a serious bereavement to Mr. Washington, whose acquaintance and regard for the deceased had begun in their childhood. Their happy union had done much to lighten the arduous duties devolving upon him in the management of his school. To his friends he had several times expressed the great comfort his family life was to him ... All our readers will join us in extending to him the warmest sympathy in this sad hour. A bright little girl, not a year old, is left to sustain with her father a loss which she can never know."

In 1885, Washington married Olivia America Davidson, who was a teacher and Lady Principal at Tuskegee. Their son, Booker T. "Baker" Washington, Jr., was born in 1887. Their second son, Ernest Davidson Washington, was born in 1889. Tragically, that same year, a fire broke out at their home, injuring Olivia and she died.

Washington wrote:

> Although the period of the school's history about which I have written in this chapter was one of constant and substantial growth, it nevertheless was during this period that the school sustained a great loss, as well as I a great personal bereavement, in the death of my beloved and faithful wife, Olivia Davidson Washington.
>
> In May, 1889, after four years of married life, she succumbed to the overtaxing duties of mother and assistant principal of the school and passed away. Her remains were laid to rest amid the tears of teachers and students. Her words of caution, advice, sympathy and encouragement were given with a judgment that rarely made an error. Her life was so full of deeds, lessons and suggestions that she will live on to bless and help the institution which she helped found as long as it is a seat of learning."
>
> Two wide-awake boys, Baker Taliaferro and Ernest Davidson, were

born to us, who were then too young to know their loss. They are now twelve and ten years of age respectively; and they, with my daughter Portia, are a source of much comfort and joy to me.

Miss Davidson came to the school almost from the very beginning, she being the next person to come after myself. I have spoken in other places of the great assistance she was in helping to build up the school in its early days. As an estimate of her worth and character, I beg to quote the words of the Rev. R.C. Bedford, a friend who knew her worth and her great help to me and to Tuskegee ... Mr. Bedford said:

"Olivia Davidson was born in Virginia, June 11, 1854. When only a little child she went with her parents to Ohio, where she grew up and received the education afforded by the common schools of that state. At an early age she went to Mississippi and there spent five years as a teacher on the large plantations.

"In 1878 she came north to her native state, and, that she might more thoroughly fit herself for the work of a teacher, she entered the Hampton Institute, from which, in one year, she graduated with great honor ... She entered the Framingham, (Mass.) Normal School, from which she graduated in two years. In August following her graduation she came to Tuskegee, Ala., to act as assistant to Prof. Washington, in the State Normal School of which he had been made principal in the July previous.

"From the very first it became evident that she had found her field of labor for life ... The story of her success has often been told, and in this brief tribute cannot be repeated.

"August 11, 1885, Miss Davidson was married to Prof. B. T. Washington, and although she at once took upon herself the cares of a very busy home life, she still retained a most important relation to the school, which no amount of warning from her friends could persuade her to drop.

"Her marriage with Mr. Washington proved a most happy one, and rarely has it been the lot of two individuals to be so thoroughly united in their life work. The coming of little Baker into the home was an occasion of great rejoicing, and the birth of another son just a few months before his mother's death only served to double the joy ...

"It would require more than human pen to tell how deep was her love for the school and how thoroughly her life was consecrated to it. Every grain of sand on all those beautiful grounds and every beam and brick in the walls must have felt the inspiration of her love.

"No more touching story could be told than that of her earnest efforts to raise money from the people about

Tuskegee and of her toilsome walks in Boston, as from house to house, and with an eloquence that was rarely refused, she sought funds to provide shelter for the hundreds of students that were flocking to the school. Her character made her especially adapted to all parts of the work in which she was engaged, and the stamp of her influence on the higher life of the school no time can ever efface.

"Among a people who make much show of religion, but often with too little of its spirit, hers was religion indeed, but with so little of show as sometimes to make her life a mystery to those who did not really know her. The blind and the poor, and above all the aged, can tell of her religion as they recall the happy Thanksgiving and Christmas times when they have sat at her table and her own hands have ministered to their wants, and when in sickness she has visited them and relieved their sufferings."

In 1890, Washington visited Fisk University, founded by Protestant Christians of the American Missionary Association. The three founders of Fisk were: John Ogden, an officer in the Union Army and a Republican Superintendent of Public Instruction; Pastor Erastus Milo Cravath, whose home was a way station on the Underground Railroad; and Edward Parmelee Smith, a Christian minister who was commissioner of Indian Affairs under Republican President Ulysses Grant.

Washington wrote:

As the address delivered at Fisk University on this occasion constitutes in a large measure the basis for many of my other addresses and much of the work I have tried to do, I give in full what the *Nashville American* said:

"An intelligent and appreciative audience composed of prominent colored citizens, students and quite a large number of white people, crowded the beautiful and commodious Fisk memorial chapel last night to hear Prof. Booker T. Washington lecture on 'Industrial Education.'

"The lecture was the first given under the auspices of the Student's Lecture Bureau of Fisk University, and was in every way a complete success. Mr. Washington is a powerful and convincing speaker. His simplicity and utter unselfishness, both in speech and action, are impressive. He speaks to the point. He does not waste words in painting beautiful pictures, but deals mostly with plain facts. Nevertheless, he is witty and caused his audience last night to laugh and applaud repeatedly the jokes and striking points of his address ... Among other things he said:

"I am exceedingly anxious that every young man and woman should keep a hopeful and cheerful spirit as to the future. Despite all of our disadvantages and hardships, ever since our forefathers set foot upon the American soil as slaves, our pathway has been marked by progress.

"Think of it: We went into slavery pagans; we came out Christians. We went into slavery pieces of property; we came out American citizens. We went into slavery without a language; we came out speaking the proud Anglo-Saxon tongue. We went into slavery with slave chains clanking about our wrists; we came out with the American ballot in our hands."

While at Fisk, Washington met Margaret Murray and invited her to teach English at Tuskegee. Her outstanding work led to her being promoted to head of women's industries.

After working tirelessly for the school, Booker and Margaret became close and married in 1892. They had no children, but Margaret was very involved in raising Portia, Booker, Jr., and Ernest.

Washington wrote:

> In October, 1893, I was married to Miss Margaret James Murray, a graduate of Fisk University, who came to Tuskegee in 1889 as a teacher. She has been in every way as much interested in the advancement of Tuskegee as myself, and fully bears her share of the responsibilities and labor, giving especial attention to the development of the girls and to work among the women through her mothers' meetings in various parts of Alabama and elsewhere.

Washington described Tuskegee:

> In the early years of the school, the anniversary exercises were held in ... the small chapel in Porter Hall, but ... friends from far and near had so increased that the chapel would no longer hold a fifth of them ...
>
> The total enrollment for the year was 400. ... All the members of that year's class were Christians. They went out as teachers of various kinds in the state of Alabama.

In 1892, Booker T. Washington recruited Robert Robinson Taylor, the first accredited African-American architect, who graduated from MIT near the top of his class. Under Taylor's direction, students at Tuskegee made the bricks and helped build over 100 campus buildings, constructing classrooms, barns, outbuildings, and in 1899, Tuskegee's impressive chapel.

Washington observed that since slaves had been forced to work so hard on plantations, once freed, some held the expectation that they did not have to work as hard, even though they were to ones benefiting from it. He taught:

> "No race can prosper till it learns that there is as much dignity in tilling a field as in writing a poem."
>
> "What is equally important, each one of the students works ... each day at some industry, in order to get skill and the love of work, so that when he goes out from the institution he is prepared to set the people with whom he goes to

labor a proper example in the matter of industry."

"Few things can help an individual more than to place responsibility on him, and to let him know that you trust him."

"To do a common thing in an uncommon way."

"To do our work so well that it will be a difficult task for anyone to improve upon what we have done."

"To live up to the high-water mark of daily duty. Whoever does this will meet with constant unexpected happiness and encouragement."

Washington encouraged students to be hard-working, courteous, behave respectably, and never put on prideful airs. He sought peaceful relations with the school's neighbors, many of whom were Southern Democrats stilling holding racist views. He wrote in *Up From Slavery: An Autobiography*, 1904:

> In the school, we made a special effort to teach our students the meaning of Christmas, and to give them lessons in its proper observance. In this we have been successful to a degree that makes me feel safe in saying that the season now has a new meaning, not only through all that immediate region, but, in a measure, wherever our graduates have gone.
>
> At the present time one of the most satisfactory features of the Christmas

and Thanksgiving season at Tuskegee is the unselfish and beautiful way in which our graduates and students spend their time in administering to the comfort and happiness of others, especially the unfortunate.

Not long ago some of our young men spent a holiday in rebuilding a cabin for a helpless colored woman who was about seventy-five years old.

He continued:

At another time I remember that I made it known in chapel one night that a very poor student was suffering from cold, because he needed a coat. The next morning two coats were sent to my office for him. I have referred to the disposition on the part of the white people in the town of Tuskegee and vicinity to help the school.

He added:

From the first, I resolved to make the school a real part of the community in which it was located. I was determined that no one should have the feeling that it was a foreign institution, dropped down in the midst of the people, for which they had no responsibility and in which they had no interest.

I noticed that the very fact that they had been asking to contribute toward the purchase of the land made them begin to feel as if it was going to be their school, to a large degree.

I noted that just in proportion as we made the white people feel that the institution was a part of the life of the community, and that, while we wanted to make friends in Boston, for example, we also wanted to make white friends in Tuskegee, and that we wanted to make the school of real service to all the people, their attitude toward the school became favorable.

He continued:

Perhaps I might add right here, what I hope to demonstrate later, that, so far as I know, the Tuskegee school at the present time has no warmer and more enthusiastic friends anywhere than it has among the white citizens of Tuskegee and throughout the state of Alabama and the entire South.

From the first, I have advised our people in the South to make friends in every straightforward, manly way with their next-door neighbor, whether he be a black man or a white man.

Washington wrote:

The man is unwise who does not cultivate in every manly way the friendship and goodwill of his next-door neighbor, whether he be black or white.

He wrote in *Sowing and Reaping* (1900):

There are six hundred thousand Negroes in the State of Alabama who are waiting to be "lifted up" ... The Tuskegee graduate should ... go out and help the masses to help themselves, while at the same time you are helping yourselves ...

We should undertake the work with brave hearts and with trained intellects and hands. We must not get discouraged. Life, in this respect, will naturally seem hard for a while, but we must not be overcome because of this, if we expect to help others and thereby help ourselves ...

Tuskegee graduates ... should make their lives an example, an inspiration to the masses among whom they cast their lot. They should teach the people how to be independent, manly, and economical in their living, and they should impress upon them the supreme importance of owning the homes in which they live.

In 1891, Washington worked with the West Virginia legislature to establish the West Virginia Colored Institute near Charleston, in the area where he had lived growing up, the Kanawha Valley. He spoke at its first commencement exercise and visited the campus often.

Washington wrote:

When persons ask me in these days how, in the midst of what sometimes seem hopelessly discouraging conditions, I can have such faith in the future of my race in this country, I remind them of the wilderness through which and out of which, a good Providence has already led us.

5. NEED FOR ECONOMIC SUCCESS

Booker T. Washington stayed focused on the need for the black race to have economic success in order to overcome racial prejudice and discrimination.

Ten years before President William Howard Taft helped found the U.S. Chamber of Commerce to counter the Marxist labor movement, Booker T. Washington founded the National Negro Business League in 1900, growing it to 600 chapters.

Washington shared his insights:

"Nothing ever comes to me, that is worth having, except as the result of hard work."

"What we should do in all our schools is to turn out fewer job seekers and more job-makers. Anyone can seek a job, but it requires a person of rare ability to create a job."

"Leaders have devoted themselves to politics, little knowing, it seems that political independence disappears without economic independence that economic independence is the foundation of political independence."

"I want to see you own land."

"The Negro has the right to study law,

but success will come to the race sooner if it produces intelligent, thrifty farmers, mechanics, to support the lawyers."

"No man, who continues to add something to the material, intellectual and moral well-being of the place in which he lives, is left long without proper reward."

"I want to see my race live such high and useful lives that they will not be merely tolerated, but they shall actually be needed and wanted because of their usefulness to the community."

He wrote in *Sowing and Reaping* (1900):

"Be not deceived; God is not mocked; for whatsoever a man soweth that shall he also reap." Again: "He which soweth sparingly shall also reap sparingly; and he which soweth bountifully shall reap also bountifully." (II Cor. ix. 15.)

These quotations are applicable to man in all the activities of life, both spiritual and material.

Our harvest is always in proportion to the amount of earnest labor that we put into our work. A farmer who puts earnest effort into his fieldwork will reap a profitable harvest ...

To attain success, we must put forth hard and honest labor ... There is no royal road. Those who think there is always fail ... Show me a man who is always grumbling, always finding fault with his condition ... and I will show you a man who does not appreciate ... (his) opportunities ... Hard labor is the keynote to success ...

No man who wishes to succeed should be afraid of doing just a little more ... If a person asks us to do a certain thing which is fair and honest, do that thing; not only do that, but do more.

Combine your force with his and win his undivided confidence. This process of overlapping ... creates a community ... "Whatsoever a man soweth that shall he also reap."

He added:

Things seen are temporal; things unseen are eternal, spiritual. Hidden things stand for character; temporal, visible things stand for reputation. After all, it is the hidden things which are most important – which stand for the highest things in the world.

Take the matter of giving ... The persons who give most generously are ... those who give quietly ... without being seen ... Quiet, unseen giving, which never reaches the ear of the public ... makes possible the best things in the world.

The student ... will find the same thing true all through his school life – that he will have to get into the habit of doing a thing because it is right, because he can put his conscience into his work. If the student fails to form this habit in the school, he will not only fail in his school life, but in his life out in the big world.

A student should not be satisfied with himself until he has grown to the point where, when simply sweeping a room, he can go into the corners and crevices and remove the hidden trash ...

It is not very hard to find people who will thoroughly clean a room which is going to be occupied, or wash a dish which is to be handled by strangers; but it is hard to find a person who will do a thing right when the eyes of the world are not likely to look upon what has been done. The cleaning of rooms and the washing of dishes have much to do with forming characters.

A man who builds a house and gives it a presentable exterior is reputed to be a conscientious and reliable contractor; but, if the real character of the man is to be known, we must tear down the house and ascertain of what the hidden timbers are composed and how they are laid. The character of the man is disclosed in the quality of his work. A man is growing when he can be relied upon to do his best seen or unseen, observed or unobserved.

Now, here, at Tuskegee Institute, for example, we want to prepare for the work of life the type of students who will put just as much energy, just as much hard work, into a lesson that is to be recited, as into one that is not to be recited ... So, it is always the hidden thing, the thing not likely to be seen, by which the man is to be judged.

> It is not difficult to find persons who will speak generous words and be unselfish in delivering a discourse before a large audience; but the way to test the real character of the person is to watch his conduct toward his neighbors, those who come into daily contact with him.

Washington's approach to blacks being fully accepted into American life was to follow the path immigrants took. German, Irish, Jewish, Polish, Italian, Chinese, Japanese, Indian, Filipino, Latin America, Scandinavian, Eastern European, Russian, and others, immigrated into the country at the bottom of the socio-economic ladder, often being met with racial discrimination.

But by hard work and pooling their efforts and resources, they became educated, started businesses, accumulated wealth, made contributions to society, became politically involved, and rose in public respect.

Washington stated:

> At the bottom of education, at the bottom of politics, even at the bottom of religion itself, there must be for our race, as for all races, an economic foundation, economic prosperity, economic independence ...
>
> ... Leaders have devoted themselves to politics, little knowing, it seems, that political independence disappears without economic independence; that economic independence is the foundation of political independence.

Washington recommended efforts to "...

concentrate all their energies on industrial education, and accumulation of wealth, and the conciliation of the South," believing that blacks would eventually gain full participation in society by showing themselves to be successful, responsible, and reliable American citizens.

Booker T. Washington taught:

> "No man who continues to add something to the material, intellectual and moral well-being of the place in which he lives is left without proper reward."

> "The world cares very little about what a man or woman knows; it is what a man or woman is able to do that counts."

> "Opportunities never come a second time, nor do they wait for our leisure."

> "We should not permit our grievances to overshadow our opportunities."

> "Success is not measured by the position one has reached in life, rather by the obstacles overcome while trying to succeed."

> "I believe that any man's life will be filled with constant and unexpected encouragement, if he makes up his mind to do his level best each day, and as nearly as possible reaching the high water mark of pure and useful living."

> "No greater injury can be done to any youth than to let him feel that because he belongs to this or that race he will be advanced in life regardless of his own merits or efforts."

6. WASHINGTON'S WISDOM

Washington wrote in *The Story of My Life*:

In the fall of 1899, a meeting was held at Huntsville, Alabama ... attended by representatives from nearly every Southern State ... Among the other subjects discussed was the Negro problem in its relation to the industrial progress of the South ...

I was invited to deliver an address. The audience was composed mainly of Southern white men, but in it was a large number of Southern white women, together with quite an attendance of colored men and women.

The address which I delivered on that occasion attracted a great deal of attention throughout the country, and for that reason I have taken the liberty of giving it in full:

"In all discussion and legislation bearing upon the presence of the Negro in America, it should be borne in mind that we are dealing with a people who were forced to come here without their consent and in the face of a most earnest protest. This gives the Negro a claim upon your sympathy and generosity that no other race can possess.

"Besides, though forced from his

native land into residence in a country that was not of his choosing, he has earned his right to the title of American citizen by obedience to the law, by patriotism and fidelity, and by the millions which his brawny arms and willing hands have added to the wealth of this country.

"In saying what I have today, although a Negro and an ex-slave myself, there is no white man whose heart is more wrapped up in every interest of the South and who loves it more dearly than is true of myself. She can have no sorrow that I do not share; she can have no prosperity that I do not rejoice in. She can commit no error that I do not deplore. She can take no step forward that I do not approve.

"Different in race, in color, in history, we can teach the world that, although thus differing, it is possible for us to dwell side by side in love, in peace, and in material prosperity. We can be one, as I believe we will be in a larger degree in the future, in sympathy, purpose, forbearance and mutual helpfulness. Let him who would embitter, who would bring strife between your race and mine, be accursed in his basket and in his store, accursed in the fruit of his body and the fruit of his land.

"No man can plan the degradation of another race without being himself degraded. The highest test of the civilization of any race is its willingness to extend a helping hand to the less fortunate.

"The South extends a protecting arm and a welcome voice to the foreigner, of all nationalities, languages and conditions, but in this I pray that you will not forget the black man at your door, whose habits you know, whose fidelity you have tested. You may make of others larger gatherers of wealth, but you cannot make of them more law-abiding, useful and God-fearing people than the Negro who has been by your side for three centuries, and whose toil in forest, field and mine has helped to make the South the land of promise and glorious possibility ...

"I have no hesitation in declaring that the great bulk of the Negro population will reside among you ...

"Here, in His wisdom, Providence has placed the Negro. Here he will remain. Here he came without a language; here he found the Anglo-Saxon tongue. Here he came in paganism; here he found the religion of Christ. Here he came in barbarism; here he found civilization. Here he came with untrained hands; here he found industry.

"If these centuries of contact with the American have done this, can you not trust to the wise Creator, aided by the efforts of the Negro himself, and your guidance, to do the remainder?...

"Your duty to the Negro will not be fulfilled until you have made of him the highest type of American citizen, in intelligence, usefulness and morality."

Booker T. Washington stated:

"The surest way to lift up ourselves, is to lift up someone else."

"If you want to lift yourself up, lift up someone else."

"There are two ways of exerting one's strength: one is pushing down, the other is pulling up."

"A race, like an individual, lifts itself up by lifting others up."

"There is no escape — man drags man down, or man lifts man up."

"You can't hold a man down without staying down with him."

"The happiest people are those who do the most for others. The most miserable are those who do the least."

"Keep in mind that service to our fellows will always be our greatest protection, and will bring our greatest happiness."

"The harder the work required on account of the ... unpopularity of the individual to be helped, the greater will be the strength and happiness gained."

"Remember that the only way to show ourselves superior to others is to excel them in kindlier impulses and more generous deeds."

7. FREDERICK DOUGLASS & WILLIAM LLOYD GARRISON

Washington wrote in *The Story of My Life & Work*:

> In the spring of 1892, at our annual commencement, we had the pleasure and the honor of a visit from Hon. Frederick Douglass, who delivered the annual address to the graduating class of that year. This was Mr. Douglass' first visit to the far South, and there was a large crowd of people from far and near to listen to the words of that grand old man. The speech was fully up to the high standard of excellence, eloquence and wisdom for which that venerable gentleman was noted.
>
> Mr. Douglass had the same idea concerning the importance and value of industrial education that I have tried to emphasize ... The more I have studied the life of Mr. Douglass, the more I have been surprised to find his far-reaching and generous grasp of the whole condition and needs of the Negro race.
>
> Years before Hampton or Tuskegee undertook industrial education, in reply to a request for advice by Mrs. Harriet Beecher Stowe as to how she could best use a certain sum of money which had been or was about to be placed in her hands, Mr.

Douglass wrote her ... as follows:

Rochester, March 8, 1853. My Dear Mrs. Stowe, You kindly informed me when at your house a fortnight ago, that you designed to do something which should permanently contribute to the improvement and elevation of the free colored people in the United States ...

To improve and elevate them, by which I mean simply to put them on an equal footing with their white fellow-countrymen in the sacred right to "Life, Liberty and the pursuit of happiness." I am for no fancied or artificial elevation, but only ask fair play ...

Free colored people will (n)ever be induced to leave this country ... The black man (unlike the Indian) loves civilization ... We are here, and here we are likely to remain ... We have grown up with this republic and see nothing in her character ... which compels the belief that we must leave the United States. If, then, we are to remain here, the question ... is ... what can be done to improve the condition of the free people of color in the United States?

The plan which I humbly submit ... is the establishment ... of an INDUSTRIAL COLLEGE in which shall be taught several important branches of the mechanic arts ... a college where colored youth can be instructed to use their hands, as well as their heads; where they can be put in possession of the means of getting a living ...

Denied the means of learning useful

trades, we are pressed into the narrowest limits to obtain a livelihood. In times past we have been the hewers of wood and drawers of water ... menial employments, but this is so no longer ...

Colored men must learn trades; must find new employments; new modes of usefulness to society ... We must become mechanics; we must build as well as live in houses; we must make as well as use furniture; we must construct bridges as well as pass over them; before we can properly live or be respected by our fellow-men.

We need mechanics as well as ministers. We need workers in iron, clay, and leather. We have orators, authors, and other professional men, but these reach only a certain class, and get respect for our race in certain select circles. To live here as we ought, we must fasten ourselves to our countrymen through their everyday, cardinal wants. We must not only be able to blacken boots, but to make them.

In *The Story of My Life & Work,* Washington copied an article from New York City's *The Outlook*:

> The Convention of the National Negro Business League, held in Boston last week, brought together upwards of a hundred delegates, representing over twenty different states ... The League was organized upon the initiative of Booker T. Washington, and his common-sense philosophy permeated most of the addresses ... The emphasis put upon the

acquiring of property sprang from the desire to lift up the manhood of the Negro race ... Economic independence is today as much needed for the further advancement of the Negro race as was emancipation from slavery ...

Even so uncompromising an opponent of materialism as Mr. William Lloyd Garrison, Jr., recognized this and emphasized it in his address: ...

"The particular word I wish to leave with you is this: Aim to be your own employers as speedily as possible. If you are farmers, do not rest until you control the land from which you gain your living.

"If you are mechanics, or traders, seek first to gain a home without a mortgage, foregoing many desirable things until you are free from debt. Independence and debt cannot long keep company. But, in the South, as in the North, possession of honestly earned property will surely bring respect and increase personal security."

Among the Negro speakers were several men who have been remarkably successful ... a slave of Jefferson Davis who is now mayor of his little town in Mississippi. The speeches of some of these men telling of early struggles were full of encouragement to Negroes everywhere. The fact that some Negroes have succeeded in business, as well as ... in literature and art ... opens the door of opportunity to all Negroes who aspire."

8. LOVE THY NEIGHBOR

The editor of *The Salvation Army's Conqueror Magazine*, Major T.C. Marshall, wrote to Booker T. Washington thanking him for his favorable comments regarding The Salvation Army's effort to minister to poor blacks in America's South.

Washington replied, July 28, 1896:

> I am very glad to hear that The Salvation Army is going to undertake work among my people in the southern states. I have always had the greatest respect for the work of The Salvation Army especially because I have noted that it draws no color line in religion ...
>
> In reaching the neglected and, I might say, outcasts of our people, I feel that your methods and work have peculiar value ... God bless you in all your unselfish Christian work for our country.

Washington expressed his views:

> In the sight of God there is no color line, and we want to cultivate a spirit that will make us forget that there is such a line anyway.

He wrote in *Up From Slavery* (1901):

> It is now long ago that I learned this lesson from General Samuel Chapman Armstrong, and resolved that I would permit no man, no matter what his color

might be, to narrow and degrade my soul by making me hate him.

With God's help, I believe that I have completely rid myself of any ill feeling toward the Southern white man for any wrong that he may have inflicted upon my race. I am made to feel just as happy now when I am rendering service to Southern white men as when the service is rendered to a member of my own race.

I pity from the bottom of my heart any individual who is so unfortunate as to get into the habit of holding race prejudice.

He wrote in *The Story of My Life and Work*:

I have long since ceased to cherish any spirit of bitterness against the Southern white people on account of the enslavement of my race.

Frederick Douglass also forgave slaveholders, as he recounted in the story of his conversion:

I was not more than thirteen years old, when I felt the need of God, as a father and protector. My religious nature was awakened by the preaching of a white Methodist minister, named Hanson. He thought that all men, great and small, bond and free, were sinners in the sight of God; that they were, by nature, rebels against His government; and that they must repent of their sins, and be reconciled to God, through Christ ...

I was, for weeks, a poor, brokenhearted mourner, traveling through the darkness and misery of doubts and fears ... I finally found that change of heart which comes by "casting all one's care" upon God, and by having faith in Jesus Christ, as the Redeemer, Friend, and Savior of those who diligently seek him ...

I gathered scattered pages of the Bible from the filthy street gutters, and washed and dried them, that ... I might get a word or two of wisdom from them ... After this, I saw the world in a new light ... I loved all mankind – slaveholders not excepted; though I abhorred slavery more than ever.

Washington wrote in *Up From Slavery* (1901):

Great men cultivate love ... only little men cherish a spirit of hatred. I learned that assistance given to the weak makes the one who gives it strong; and that oppression of the unfortunate makes one weak.

He noted in an address on Abraham Lincoln to the Republican Club of New York City, February 12, 1909:

"One man cannot hold another man down in the ditch without remaining down in the ditch with him."

He wrote in *Sowing and Reaping* (1900):

Success or failure depends very largely upon the side of life we choose. Every person desires to choose either the higher or the lower side of life, and with tie choice a determination is made to live for higher or for lower things.

It is evident that: if a person chooses the higher side of life, and lives up to his choice, he will succeed; but, on the other hand, if he chooses the lower side of life he will fail. "The way of the transgressor is hard." There is no escape. We should always strive to see things from the higher-life point of view.

Instead of picking flaws in the character, and making unjust and uncalled for criticisms upon our neighbors and their work, we should encourage them in order that they may improve. If there is any good in a person, let us seek to find it; the evil will take care of itself.

One of the greatest temptations young people have, who live on the lower side of life, is to engage in profane, vulgar, and boisterous conversation. The nature of a person's conversation largely determines what he is.

Young people especially should seek to converse with persons whose conversation, whose thought, is pure and refined. The influence of unhealthy conversation is so great that nothing can counteract the harm it does a person's character.

If a young person finds himself associated with a person of either sex who has no regard for healthy thinking and pure expression, he should rid himself of the association. If he does not do so, he will eventually fall to the level of his companion. It is true that "birds of a feather flock together."

Young as well as old people should avoid the habit of speaking ill of others. The person who is always talking about somebody else must necessarily possess a low and cowardly nature ... The gossiper and vilifier usually gets the worst of it in the end. So, above all things, avoid the habit of talking about others.

Evil association is another thing that will injure the reputation of a person. Nothing is so likely to injure the reputation of a young person as associating with persons who are low and vulgar in their conduct and speech. Young people, especially, should never associate with persons whose influence will drag them down. If their companionship is not a help it should be abandoned, because in all conditions of life "evil communications corrupt good manners."

The tendency of our nature, at the very best, is downward. If we do not associate with the best people possible in our condition of life, shame and degradation will inevitably be our portion. We should seek always the companionship of people who live high and think high and act high.

Show me a person who entertains high thoughts, endorses high actions, and who possesses a broad and generous nature, and I will show you a person who is respected and beloved by his neighbors.

Washington stated:

"Character, not circumstances, makes the man."

"You may fill your heads with knowledge or skillfully train your hands, but unless it is based upon high upright character, upon a true heart, it will amount to nothing."

9. CHRISTIAN CHARITY & DONORS TO TUSKEGEE

Booker T. Washington became friends with the leading men of his day, including President William McKinley, President Theodore Roosevelt and President William H. Taft.

He developed relationships with entrepreneurs, philanthropists and industrialists, such as Standard Oil's John D. Rockefeller and Henry Huttleston Rogers; George Eastman, inventor and founder of Kodak; Philadelphia Quaker Anna T. Jeanes; Robert Curtis Ogden; Collis Potter Huntington; William Henry Baldwin; Steel industrialist Andrew Carnegie; and Sears, Roebuck & Company President Julius Rosenwald.

Rosenwald, a noted Jewish philanthropist, funded a pilot program of over 100 elementary schools, designed and operated by Tuskegee. Rosenwald and Carnegie took a "matching fund" approach, expanding to 4,977 schools, 217 teacher homes and 163 shop buildings in 15 States. Tuskegee's Agricultural College on Wheels, taught over 2,000 farmers in 28 States.

Washington was thankful for privileged rich people who generously gave to support the work at Tuskegee (*Up From Slavery*, 1901):

> The more I come into contact with wealthy people, the more I believe that

they are growing in the direction of looking upon their money simply as an instrument which God has placed in their hand for doing good with ...

I never go to the office of Mr. John D. Rockefeller, who more than once has been generous to Tuskegee, without being reminded of this.

The close, careful, and minute investigation that he always makes in order to be sure that every dollar that he gives will do the most good – an investigation that is just as searching as if he were investing money in a business enterprise - convinces me that the growth in this direction is most encouraging.

Washington added:

In the city of Boston, I have rarely called upon an individual for funds that I have not been thanked for calling, usually before I could get an opportunity to thank the donor for the money ... The donors seem to feel, in a large degree, that an honor is being conferred upon them in their being permitted to give ...

Nowhere else have I met with, in so large a measure, this fine and Christ-like spirit as in the city of Boston, although there are many notable instances of it outside that city. I repeat my belief that the world is growing in the direction of giving.

Washington lived out Proverbs 18:16 (NASB) which states:

A person's gift makes room for him

and brings him before great people.

Washington was grateful for the generosity of Christian churches, as he wrote in *Up From Slavery*, 1901:

> When speaking directly in the interests of the Tuskegee Institute, I usually arrange, sometime in advance, a series of meetings in important centers. This takes me before churches, Sunday schools, Christian Endeavor Societies, and men's and women's clubs. When doing this I sometimes speak before as many as four organizations in a single day.

He added:

> In my efforts to get money (for Tuskegee) I have often been surprised at the patience and deep interest of the ministers, who are besieged on every hand and at all hours of the day for help.
>
> If no other consideration had convinced me of the value of the Christian life, the Christ-like work which the Church of all denominations in America has done during the last thirty-five years for the elevation of the black man would have made me a Christian.
>
> In a large degree it has been the pennies, the nickels, and the dimes which have come from the Sunday schools, the Christian Endeavor societies, and the missionary societies, as well as from the church proper, that have helped to elevate the Negro at so rapid a rate.

Washington addressed students, as recorded in *Sowing and Reaping* (1900):

> You have all, doubtless, read that portion of the Scriptures which tells of the woman who touched the hem of Christ's garment, and thus showed her faith. The act in itself was a little thing; and yet this power of human confidence is something that we do not always fully understand and appreciate. Here we have an example of one person merely touching another, and one of them becoming healed of her infirmities simply by reason of that contact.
>
> How often do we come in contact with men and women, in whose presence we may be only a short time, and are made better, are lifted up, as it were! And all of us are constantly having the opportunity of coming into contact with such persons. Every time human life touches human life one person is made better or worse by the contact.
>
> We are always surrounded by persons who are sick, diseased by reason of their wickedness, people who fall into temptation, who are sick, down and discouraged in the race of life, weary of living, because of some misfortune of their own making. There are others who want to be made whole again, and be rid of their ignorance; others want to be helped because of their poverty and misery, people who are suffering in one way or another, craving for the health and strength that we can give them.

We have the power to make these people strong, to heal them of their infirmities, even as Christ had when he lived among men. We have the opportunity in our business life constantly.

We can often heal these necessitous people by a simple visit, by speaking a kind word, by giving them something for which they most crave; if they be sick, by giving them a small bunch of flowers. There are thousands of ways in which we can heal those afflicted in mind or body.

You, students of Tuskegee, will go out among a class of people who are cast down, discouraged by the many disadvantages and infirmities of life; people craving for the health that you can give them.

The question, then, presents itself to every teacher, every captain prepared for leadership: Are you going to live such a life that, when these people come in contact with you, look you in the face, they will be made stronger and better by the contact? There are persons whose lives are so much like that of Christ's, who have so much genuine Christianity in them, that we cannot come in contact with them, we cannot even steal a glance at their faces, without being made stronger and better.

It is said that on one cold wintry day, when the rain was falling, just such a day as to make one feel despondent, Phillips Brooks was walking through one of the streets of Boston. Those who looked into his face discovered a ray of sunshine there. Why? Because that man was so full "of the milk of human kindness," so overflowing with love of humanity, that no man, however degraded, could look into his face without being helped, without feeling that he had a place in the great heart of Phillips Brooks.

It is true that Phillips Brooks was an Episcopalian, but no denominational ties could bind him; he was a pastor of a certain church, but every man in Boston loved him, because he had the healing power in him.

Now, if those who annually go out from the schools of our great country, wherever they go, will carry with them something of this healing power, this power that will cure men merely by letting them come in contact with them, even in the slightest manner, if they will catch something of the Christ like spirit, we can have a heaven, as it were on earth. I do not believe in waiting for the heaven of the future. If we imitate the life of Christ as nearly as possible, heaven will come about more and more right here on earth.

No person can expend any life force without receiving life force in return. When we give out this spirit, something of this healing power, we receive in return more strength for ourselves, for virtue, like vice, thrives upon what it feeds.

10. VIEWS ON THE BIBLE

Booker T. Washington believed that to be great, one should read the Bible (*The Booker T. Washington Papers*, Vol. 3: 1889-1895, ed., Louis R. Harlan, Univ. of Illinois Press, 1974):

> As a rule, a person should get into the habit of reading his Bible. You never read in history of any great man whose influence has been lasting, who has not been a reader of the Bible.
>
> Take Abraham Lincoln and Gladstone. Their lives show that they have been readers of the Bible. If you wish to properly direct your mind and necessarily your lives, begin by reading the book of all books.
>
> Read your Bible every day, and you will find how healthily you will grow.

On May 24, 1900, Booker T. Washington delivered the address in Ohio, "The Place of the Bible in the Uplifting of the Negro Race":

> The men doing the vital things of life are those who read the Bible and are Christians and not ashamed to let the world know it.

He wrote:

> Those who have accomplished the greatest results are those ... who never

grow excited or lose self-control, but are always calm, self-possessed, patient and polite.

He believed a religious life was key to freedom, usefulness and honor, writing in *Putting the Most into Life* (NY: Thomas Y. Crowell & Co., 1906, ch. "Making Religion a Vital Part of Living," p. 23-25):

> Educated men and women, especially those who are in college, very often get the idea that religion is fit only for the common people. No young man or woman can make a greater error than this ...
>
> My observation has taught me that the people who stand for the most in the educational and commercial world and in the uplifting of the people are in some real way connected with the religious life of the people among whom they reside. This being true we ought to make the most of our religious life ...

He continued:

> First the habit of regular attendance at some religious service should be cultivated. This is one of the outward helps toward inward grace ...
>
> As you value your spiritual life, see to it that you do not lose the spirit of reverence for the Most High ... Do not mistake denominationalism for reverence and religion. Religion is life, denominationalism is an aid to life.

He added:

> Systematic reading and prayerful study of the Bible is the second outward

help which I would commend to those whom I wish to see make the most of their spiritual life.

Many people regard the Bible as a wonderful piece of literature only ... Nowhere in all literature can be found a finer bit of oratory than St. Paul's defense before King Agrippa.

But praiseworthy as this kind of study is, I do not believe it is sufficient. The Bible should be read as a daily guide to right living and as a daily incentive to positive Christian service ...

Washington went on:

To live the real religious life is in some measure to share the character of God. The word 'atonement,' which occurs in the Bible again and again, means literally at-one-ment.

To be at one with God is to be like God. Our real religious striving, then, should be to become one with God, sharing with Him in our poor human way His qualities and attributes. To do this, we must get the inner life, the heart right, and we shall then become stronger where we have been weak, wise where we have been foolish ...

He concluded:

We must learn to incorporate God's laws into our thoughts and words and acts. Frequent reference is made in the Bible to the freedom that comes from being a Christian.

> A man is free just in proportion as he learns to live within God's laws ... As we learn God's laws and grow into His likeness we shall find our reward in this world in a life of usefulness and honor. To do this is to have found the kingdom of God, which is the kingdom of character and righteousness and peace.

Washington stated May 24, 1900:

> The work today is to make religion the vital part of the Negro's life. But this is a stupendous task, as there is a nation of Negros ...
>
> Just remember that the Negro came out of Africa a few centuries ago ... chains upon his ankles and wrists. He came out of that ... with a hammer and a saw in his hands and a Bible in his hands. No man can read the Bible and be lazy. Christianity increases a man's ... capacity for labor. The Negro doesn't run from the Bible, either.

Washington stated:

> To be one with God is to be like God. Our real religious striving then, should be to become one with God; sharing with Him in our poor humble way His qualities and attributes."

11. ATLANTA EXPOSITION

Booker T. Washington addressed the racially mixed crowd at the International Exposition in Atlanta, September 18, 1895:

> A ship lost at sea for many days suddenly sighted a friendly vessel. From the mast of the unfortunate vessel was seen a signal, "Water, water; we die of thirst!" The answer from the friendly vessel at once came back, "Cast down your bucket where you are."

To understand the significance of Booker T. Washington's story, some background is needed.

On Columbus' third of his four attempts to reach India and China, he sailed south along the west coast of Africa before heading west across the Atlantic Ocean. His voyage was the first ever to experience and record the "doldrums" – a dangerous condition near the equator where there is intense heat and no wind.

This region was later named "horse latitudes" by subsequent unfortunate sailors headed to the New World. Stranded in the "doldrums" for weeks, sailors baked in the hot sun and ran short of drinking water, as the salty ocean was undrinkable. To save what little water they had left, they reportedly pushed overboard the horses they were transporting.

In 1498, after Columbus drifted aimlessly for eight days in the doldrums, and running out of drinking water, he prayed and vowed that if the winds returned, he would name the first land he saw after the Holy Trinity. The winds returned and on July 31, 1498, Columbus sighted an island off the coast of Venezuela which coincidentally had three peaks rising from the bay.

He obtained fresh water for his sailors and in the process was the first European to see South America. Columbus named the island Trinidad in honor of the Holy Trinity.

The doldrums were described by English poet Samuel Taylor Coleridge in his lyrical poem, "The Rime of the Ancient Mariner," 1798.

A ship was lost in the ice of Antarctica but was providentially led out of it by a large seabird, an albatross, whose wing-span can reach 12-feet. Disregarding its help, the captain shot the albatross, and brought a curse upon them: "With my crossbow, I shot the albatross."

Though they escaped the ice, the ship was later stranded in the doldrums near the equator as punishment for the captain killing the albatross:

> Day after day, day after day,
> We stuck, nor breath nor motion;
> As idle as a painted ship
> Upon a painted ocean.
> Water, water, everywhere,
> And all the boards did shrink;
> Water, water, everywhere,

> Nor any drop to drink.
> The very deep did rot – Oh Christ!
> That ever this should be.
> Yea, slimy things did crawl with legs,
> Upon the slimy sea.

The dying crew blamed the captain and hung the dead albatross around his neck:

> Ah! Well a-day!
> What evil looks
> Had I from old and young!
> Instead of the cross, the albatross
> About my neck was hung.

When the captain finally repented of his misdeed, the dead albatross fell from off his neck, and the wind supernaturally began to blow:

> The air is cut away before,
> And closes from behind.

When he sighted land, he thought it was a dream:

> Oh! Dream of joy!
> Is this indeed
> The light-house top I see?
> Is this the hill? Is this the kirk (church)?
> Is this mine own country?
> We drifted o'er the harbor-bar,
> And I with sobs did pray—
> O let me be awake, my God!
> Or let me sleep alway.

After reaching land, the captain then spent the rest of his life wandering and telling the story of his crime, repentance and salvation.

Samuel Taylor Coleridge concluded his poem:
> He prayeth best, who loveth best
> All things both great and small;
> For the dear God who loveth us,
> He made and loveth all.

The doldrums were referred to by Booker T. Washington, the President of Tuskegee Institute, in his famous address at the International Exposition in Atlanta, September 18, 1895, attended by President Grover Cleveland.

As recorded in *Up From Slavery* (1901), Booker T. Washington urged racial reconciliation:

> Atlanta was literally packed, at the time, with people from all parts of the country, and with representatives of foreign governments, as well as with military and civic organizations ...
>
> The afternoon papers had forecasts of the next day's proceedings in flaring headlines. All this tended to add to my burden. I did not sleep much that night ...
>
> The next morning, before day, I went carefully over what I planned to say. I also kneeled down and asked God's blessing upon my effort.
>
> Right here, perhaps, I ought to add that I make it a rule never to go before an audience, on any occasion, without asking the blessing of God upon what I want to say ...

Washington continued:

> A ship lost at sea for many days suddenly sighted a friendly vessel. From the mast of the unfortunate vessel was seen a signal, "Water, water; we die of thirst!" The answer from the friendly vessel at once came back, "Cast down your bucket where you are" ...
>
> A second time the signal, "Water, water; send us water!" ran up from the distressed vessel, and was answered, "Cast down your bucket where you are."
>
> And a third and fourth signal for water was answered, "Cast down your bucket where you are."
>
> The captain of the distressed vessel, at last heading the injunction, cast down his bucket, and it came up full of fresh, sparkling water from the mouth of the Amazon River.

The Amazon River is considered the longest river in the world, stretching across 4,345 miles. Where it enters the Atlantic Ocean, it is approximately 110 miles wide, discharging 7 to 11 million cubic feet of fresh water per second, which is 20 percent of the world's river water entering the ocean. The Amazon River is so powerful that it pushes a stream of drinkable water, 100 miles wide, out into the ocean for nearly 300 miles.

This is where the ship was that Washington cited in his speech. He continued his Atlanta address:

> To those of my race who depend on bettering their condition in a foreign land or who underestimate the importance of

cultivating friendly relations with the Southern white man, who is their next-door neighbor, I would say: "Cast down your bucket where you are" - cast it down in making friends in every manly way of the people of all races by whom we are surrounded ...

He continued:

To those of the white race who look to the incoming of those of foreign birth and strange tongue and habits of the prosperity of the South, were I permitted I would repeat what I say to my own race: "Cast down your bucket where you are." Cast it down among the eight millions of Negroes whose habits you know, whose fidelity and love you have tested.

He concluded:

Casting down your bucket among my people, helping and encouraging them as you are doing on these grounds, and, with education of had, hand and heart, you will find that they will buy your surplus land, make blossom the waste places in your fields, and run your factories.

While doing this, you can be sure in the future, as in the past, that you and your families will be surrounded by the most patient, faithful, law-abiding, and unresentful people that the world has seen ...

As we have proved our loyalty to you in the past ... so in the future, in our humble way, we shall stand by you with a devotion that no foreigner can approach, ready to lay down our lives, if need be, in defense of yours, interlacing our industrial, commercial, civil, and religious life with yours in a way that shall make the interests of both races one.

In all things that are purely social we can be as separate as the fingers, yet one as the hand in all things essential to mutual progress ... In your effort to work out the great and intricate problem which God has laid at the doors of the South, you shall have at all times the patient, sympathetic help of my race ...

Yet far above and beyond material benefits will be that higher good, that let us pray God will come, in a blotting out of sectional differences and racial animosities ...

This coupled with our material prosperity, will bring into our beloved South a new heaven and a new earth.

Booker T. Washington lectured from New Hampshire to California, Minnesota to Florida, raising money for the school. On January 23, 1906, he spoke at New York's Carnegie Hall, along with the great orators Mark Twain, Ambassador Joseph Hodges Choate, and Hampton Institute trustee Robert Curtis Ogden.

Washington's address the Memorial Hall in Columbus, Ohio, May 24, 1900, was described in *The Booker T. Washington Papers*, Vol. 5: 1899-1900, (Univ. of Illinois Press, 1976, p. 543-544):

> Dr. Washington walked on the stage at Memorial Hall with a firm, confident

tread, as one sure of his ground ... His shoulders are broad and six feet of stature gives strength and poise to command respect. His hair is close cut and gives him the aspect of a war dog with all its tenacious fighting spirit.

The eyes, however, gleam with kindliness and they temper the appearance of the latent fighting forces ... His jaw has the firmness of one who has the courage to stand by his convictions ...

The description continued:

"It's easy to see how that man succeeds," whispered a delegate to the Bible students' conference after looking at the speaker. John R. Mott, general secretary of the student movement of North America, presided at the afternoon meeting at Memorial Hall ... Mr. Mott announced Dr. Washington's subject as "The Place of the Bible in the Uplifting of the Negro Race."

The description ended:

Dr. Washington began his address after a quartet sang. He spoke of the ninety-one Y.M.C.A. organizations for colored youths; of the 5000 colored men studying the Bible, and of the 640 Bible students at Tuskegee, and pointed these as living examples of the progress of the Negro. He pleaded for two more secretaries to teach Bible in the South-land.

12. GEORGE WASHINGTON CARVER

George Washington Carver was also recruited to teach at Tuskegee. He was born a slave toward the end of the Civil War. His father, who belonged to the next farm over, was killed in a log hauling accident.

Shortly after the Civil War, while still an infant, bushwhackers from the Democrat South kidnapped George, along with his mother and sister.

Moses Carver, a German immigrant, sent friends to track down the thieves and offer to trade his best horse to retrieve them.

Told to leave the horse and come back later, the thieves only left baby George lying on the ground, sick with the whooping cough, an illness which permanently effected his physical health. George never saw his mother and sister again.

Illness claimed the lives of his two other sisters, and they were buried on the old Carver farm. George and his older brother, Jim, were raised the farm in Diamond Grove, Missouri, by "Uncle" Moses and "Aunt" Sue Carver, who were childless. Jim died of smallpox, and George suffered from poor health as a child.

George stayed near the house helping with

chores, learning to cook, clean, sew, mend and wash laundry, skills that he would later use to support himself. His recreation was to spend time in the woods. The Carvers supported George's decision to leave home to attend school in Neosho, Missouri. He paid his own tuition by doing odd jobs.

He wrote in *A Brief Sketch of My Life*, 1922:

> I would never allow anyone to give me money, no difference how badly I needed it. I wanted literally to earn my living.

In the intervening years, George Carver worked his way through grade school and high school, cooking and doing laundry, drifting from Missouri to Kansas in 1878. He homesteaded in western Kansas in the 1880s, then traveled to Iowa where he studied art at Simpson College.

One of his paintings received an honorable mention in the Chicago World's Fair in 1893.

He transferred to Iowa State College of Agricultural and Mechanical Arts where he worked his way through school, earning a Bachelor of Agriculture degree and a Master of Science degree in plant diseases and mycology. Iowa State them hired him as staff to be a teacher.

In the Spring of 1896, George Washington Carver received an invitation from Booker T. Washington to join the staff of the Tuskegee Institute in Alabama.

> Tuskegee Institute seeks to provide education — a means for survival to those who attend. Our students are poor,

often starving. They travel miles of torn roads, across years of poverty.

We teach them to read and write, but words cannot fill stomachs. They need to learn how to plant and harvest crops ...

I cannot offer you money, position or fame. The first two you have. The last, from the place you now occupy, you will no doubt achieve. These things I now ask you to give up.

I offer you in their place work — hard, hard work — the challenge of bringing people from degradation, poverty and waste to full manhood.

Carver wrote back, May 16, 1896:

My dear Sir, I am just in receipt of yours of the 13th inst., and hasten to reply.

I am looking forward to a very busy, pleasant and profitable time at your college and shall be glad to cooperate with you in doing all I can through Christ who strengtheneth me to better the condition of our people.

Some months ago, I read your stirring address delivered at Chicago and I said amen to all you said, furthermore you have the correct solution to the "race problem" ...

Providence permitting, I will be there in November. God bless you and your work, –Geo. W. Carver.

As mentioned earlier, Booker T. Washington's

solution of the "race problem" was to gain respect through economic independence — the pathway taken by every new wave of immigrants, ie., German, Irish, Jewish, Polish, Italian, Asian, and others. Immigrants arrived on the shores of America at the bottom of the social ladder and were met with racial discrimination. They lived in poor neighborhoods, worked hard, got educated, started businesses, and pooled their resources.

As they gradually accumulated wealth and made positive contributions to society, they rose in public respect. In *The Story of My Life & Work*, Washington wrote:

> If we make ourselves intelligent, industrious, economical and virtuous, of value to the community in which we live, we can and will work out our own salvation right here in the South ...
>
> Those who fought for the freedom of the slaves performed their duty heroically and well, but ... mere fiat of law cannot make an ignorant voter an intelligent voter; cannot make a dependent man an independent man; cannot make one citizen respect another. These results will come to the Negro, as to all races, by beginning at the bottom and gradually working up to the highest possibilities of his nature.
>
> In the economy of God there is but one standard by which an individual can succeed.

Booker T. Washington stated:

> There must be for our race, as

for all races ... economic prosperity, economic independence ... Political independence disappears without economic independence.

He recommended they

... concentrate all their energies on industrial education, and accumulation of wealth, and the conciliation of the South.

Booker T. Washington wrote in *The Future of the American Negro* (1899):

Educated Negroes should give more attention to the history of their race ... and ... mark its progress ... so that from year to year, instead of looking back with regret, we can point to our children the rough path through which we grew strong and great.

We have a bright and striking example in the history of the Jews in this and other countries. There is, perhaps, no race that has suffered so much, not so much in America as in some of the countries in Europe. But these people have clung together ... had a certain amount of unity, pride, and love of race; and, as the years go on, they will be more and more influential in this country, where they were once despised, and looked upon with scorn and derision.

It is largely because the Jewish race has had faith in itself. Unless the Negro learns more and more to imitate the Jew in these matters, to have faith in himself, he cannot expect to have any high degree of success.

He wrote:

> I have begun everything with the idea that I could succeed, and I never had much patience with the multitudes of people who are always ready to explain why one cannot succeed ...
>
> I have learned that success is to be measured not so much by the position that one has reached in life as by the obstacles which he has overcome while trying to succeed.

Frederick Douglass, the African-American Republican advisor to Abraham Lincoln, expressed a similar view in 1859:

> Self-made men ... are the men who owe little or nothing to birth, relationship, friendly surroundings; to wealth inherited or to early approved means of education; who are what they are, without the aid of any of the favoring conditions by which other men usually rise in the world and achieve great results ...
>
> The man who will get up will be helped up; and the man who will not get up will be allowed to stay down ...
>
> Give the Negro fair play and let him alone ... Where circumstances do most for men, there a man will do the least for himself ... His doing makes or unmakes him ...
>
> My theory of self-made men is, then,

simply this; that they are men of work ... Honest labor faithfully, steadily and persistently pursued, is the best, if not the only, explanation of their success.

In the fall of 1896, George Washington Carver surprised the staff by announcing his plans to give up his promising future there and join the staff of the Tuskegee Institute in Alabama. The staff at Iowa State showed Carver their appreciation by purchasing him a going away present – a microscope, which he used extensively throughout his career.

At Tuskegee, George assembled an Agricultural Department. He visited nearby farmers and would teach them farming techniques, such as crop rotation, fertilization, and erosion prevention. He noticed that the soil was depleted due to years of repeated cotton growth and produced very poorly.

During this time, an insect called the boll weevil swept through the South, destroying cotton crops and leaving farmers devastated. George showed the farmers the benefits of planting legumes, such as peanuts, which replenish the soil with nitrogen.

Farmers heeded Carver's advice but soon had more peanuts than the market wanted, as peanuts were primarily used as animal feed. He determined to increase the market for peanuts by discovering and popularizing hundreds of uses for them, which helped to revolutionize the South's economy. He did the same for the soybean, sweet potato, pecan, cowpea, wild plum, and okra.

George credited Divine Inspiration for giving

him ideas regarding how to perform experiments.

In the summer of 1920, the Young Men's Christian Association of Blue Ridge, North Carolina, invited Professor Carver to speak at their summer school for the southern states.

Dr. Willis D. Weatherford, President of Blue Ridge, introduced him as the speaker. With his high voice surprising the audience, Dr. Carver exclaimed humorously:

> I always look forward to introductions as opportunities to learn something about myself ...

He continued:

> Years ago, I went into my laboratory and said, "Dear Mr. Creator, please tell me what the universe was made for?"
>
> The Great Creator answered, "You want to know too much for that little mind of yours. Ask for something more your size, little man."
>
> Then I asked, "Please, Mr. Creator, tell me what man was made for."
>
> Again, the Great Creator replied, "You are still asking too much. Cut down on the extent and improve the intent" ...
>
> So then I asked, "Please, Mr. Creator, will you tell me why the peanut was made?"
>
> "That's better, but even then it's infinite. What do you want to know about the peanut?"
>
> "Mr. Creator, can I make milk out

of the peanut?"

"What kind of milk do you want? Good Jersey milk or just plain boarding house milk?"

"Good Jersey milk." And then the Great Creator taught me to take the peanut apart and put it together again. And out of the process have come forth all these products!

Among the numerous products displayed was a bottle of good Jersey milk. Three and-a-half ounces of peanuts produced one pint of rich milk or one quart of raw "skim" milk, called boarding house "blue john" milk.

On January 21, 1921, Carver addressed the United States House Ways and Means Committee on behalf of the United Peanut Growers Association on the use of peanuts to improve Southern economy. He expounded on the many potential uses of the peanut as a means to improve the Southern economy.

Initially given only ten minutes to speak, Carver so enthralled the committee that the Chairman said, "Go ahead Brother. Your time is unlimited!"

He spoke for one hour and forty-five minutes, explaining the many food products that could be derived from peanuts:

> If you go to the first chapter of Genesis, we can interpret very clearly, I think, what God intended when he said, 'Behold, I have given you every herb that bears seed. To you it shall be

meat.' This is what He means about it. It shall be meat. There is everything there to strengthen and nourish and keep the body alive and healthy.

The Committee Chairman asked Carver:

"Dr. Carver, how did you learn all of these things?"

He answered, "From an old book."

"What book?" asked the Chairman.

Carver replied, "The Bible."

The Chairman inquired, "Does the Bible tell about peanuts?"

"No, Sir" Carver replied, "But it tells about the God who made the peanut. I asked Him to show me what to do with the peanut, and He did."

Carver addressed 500 people at the Women's Board of Domestic Missions, November 19, 1924:

God is going to reveal to us things He never revealed before if we put our hands in His. No books ever go into my laboratory. The thing I am to do and the way are revealed to me the moment I am inspired to create something new.

Without God to draw aside the curtain, I would be helpless. Only alone can I draw close enough to God to discover His secrets.

In 1928, Dr. George Washington Carver worded that sentiment in a spiritual light:

Human need is really a great spiritual vacuum which God seeks to fill ... With one hand in the hand of a fellow man in need and the other in the hand of Christ, He could get across the vacuum ... Then the passage, "I can do all things through Christ which strengthens me," came to have real meaning.

On July 10, 1924, George Washington Carver wrote to James Hardwick:

> God cannot use you as He wishes until you come into the fullness of His Glory. Do not get alarmed, my friend, when doubts creep in. That is old Satan.
>
> Pray, pray, pray. Oh, my friend, I am praying that God will come in and rid you entirely of self so you can go out after souls right, or rather have souls seek the Christ in you. This is my prayer for you always.

Though from a disadvantaged background, George did not let this pull him down into self-pity, bitterness, or yielding to a hateful victimhood mentality.

Carver wrote to YMCA official Jack Boyd in Denver, Colorado, March 1, 1927:

> My beloved friend, keep your hand in that of the Master, walk daily by His side, so that you may lead others into the realms of true happiness, where a religion of hate, (which poisons both body and soul) will be unknown, having in its place the "Golden Rule" way, which is the "Jesus Way" of life, will reign supreme ...
>
> Then, we can walk and talk with Jesus momentarily, because we will

be attuned to His will and wishes, thus making the Creation story of the world non-debatable as to its reality.

The "Golden Rule" is what Jesus taught in the Sermon on the Mount (Matthew 7:12; Luke 6:31):

> In everything, then, do to others as you would have them do to you. For this is the essence of the Law and the prophets.

The Jesus Way was one of forgiveness, as taught in Matthew chapter 6:

> After this manner therefore pray ... Forgive us our trespasses as we forgive those who trespass against us ... For if ye forgive men their trespasses, your heavenly Father will also forgive you:
>
> But if ye forgive not men their trespasses, neither will your Father forgive your trespasses.

Jesus taught in Matthew 18:32-35

> Then the master summoned him and declared, 'You wicked servant! I forgave all your debt because you begged me. Shouldn't you have had mercy on your fellow servant, just as I had on you?'
>
> In anger his master turned him over to the jailers to be tortured, until he should repay all that he owed. That is how My heavenly Father will treat each of you unless you forgive your brother from your heart.

In contrast to "critical race theory" and the "cancel culture," Jesus taught:

> But I say unto you, love your enemies, bless them that curse you, do good to them that hate you, and pray for them which despitefully use you, and persecute you. (Matthew 5:44)

Paul taught in Romans 12:17-21:

> Do not repay anyone evil for evil. Be careful to do what is right in the eyes of everyone. If it is possible, as far as it depends on you, live at peace with everyone.
>
> Do not take revenge, my dear friends, but leave room for God's wrath, for it is written: "It is mine to avenge; I will repay," says the Lord. (ref. Deut. 32:35)
>
> On the contrary: "If your enemy is hungry, feed him; if he is thirsty, give him something to drink. In doing this, you will heap burning coals on his head, and the Lord will reward you" (ref. Prov. 25:21-22) Do not be overcome by evil, but overcome evil with good.

The Book of Ezekiel 18:20, states:

> The son shall not be punished for his father's sins.

Carver continued his letter to Jack Boyd, March 1, 1927:

> God, my beloved friend, is infinite, the highest embodiment of love. We are finite, surrounded and often filled with hate. We can only understand the infinite as we lose the finite and take on the infinite.
>
> My dear friend, my friendship to

you cannot possibly mean what yours does to me ... You help me to see God through another angle ... Most sincerely yours, G.W. Carver.

Carver addressed Congress and met with Presidents Theodore Roosevelt, Calvin Coolidge, and Franklin Roosevelt. He was offered jobs by Henry Ford and Thomas Edison. He received correspondence from business and world leaders, including Harvey Kellogg, Stalin, and Mahatma Gandhi. On March 24, 1925, Carver wrote to Robert Johnson, an employee of Chesley Enterprises of Ontario:

Thank God I love humanity; complexion doesn't interest me one single bit.

In 1939, George Washington Carver was awarded the Roosevelt Medal, with the declaration:

To a scientist humbly seeking the guidance of God and a liberator to men of the white race as well as the black.

Carver died January 5, 1943. That same year, Senator Harry S Truman sponsored the bill to designate Carver's birthplace as a National Monument — the first national monument dedicated to an African-American.

In 1948 and 1998, the U.S. Post Office issued postage stamps honoring Carver. In 1951, George Washington Carver and Booker T. Washington had their image placed on a half-dollar.

13. CHRISTIANITY AT TUSKEGEE

Daily life at Tuskegee was permeated by active religion, including Sunday preaching services and Sunday school classes, daily evening chapel devotionals and a "Week of Prayer" held for two weeks every January. Students helped out at community churches; ran a Y.M.C.A.; cared for sick, needy, and elderly in the area; and staffed a Humane Society for the care of animals.

Washington began a Bible training school in 1893:

> While the institution is in no sense denominational, we have a department known as the Phelps Hall Bible Training School, in which a number of students are prepared for the ministry and other forms of Christian work, especially work in the country districts.

> In the school we made a special effort to teach our students the meaning of Christmas, and to give them lessons in its proper observance ... The Season now has a new meaning, not only through all that immediate region, but ... wherever our graduates have gone.

Washington wrote in *Up From Slavery*, 1901:

> While a great deal of stress is laid upon the industrial side of the work at Tuskegee, we do not neglect or overlook in any

degree the religious and spiritual side.

The school is strictly undenominational, but it is thoroughly Christian, and the spiritual training of the students is not neglected. Our preaching service, prayer meetings, Sunday school, Christian Endeavor Society, Young Men's Christian Association, and various missionary organizations testify to this.

In *The Story of My Life & Work*, he wrote:

The whole of my time, thought and energy, for the past eighteen years, have been devoted to the building up of this Institute ... in its various departments, agricultural, mechanical, domestic science, nurse training, musical, Bible training, and academic ...

The Bible Training Department was established in 1893. The desire for increased opportunities for those who wish to fit themselves for the ministry, or other forms of Christian work in the South, had been long felt.

To meet this need, a generous lady in New York erected at Tuskegee a building called Phelps Hall ... containing a chapel, library, reading room, office, three recitation rooms and forty sleeping rooms, to be used as a Bible School ... one of the most beautiful and desirable buildings on the school grounds.

The instruction is wholly undenominational. It is the aim of this new department to help all denominations, and not to antagonize any. The Bible School is not in opposition to any other theological work now being done, but it is simply a means of helping ...

The members of the Bible School are required to do mission work on the Sabbath in the neighboring churches — preaching and teaching in the Sunday Schools whenever their services are needed — and to make weekly reports in writing of the work done.

It is not necessary to have a special call to the ministry to enter the Bible School at Tuskegee. Many who desire to do only missionary work or to become intelligent teachers of the Bible in the Sunday Schools, will be greatly benefited and helped; indeed, quite a few of those who are now members of this department are fitting themselves for this kind of work.

The demand for an educated ministry is growing throughout the South, and those who expect to preach must prepare themselves for the work.

This department was established for the express purpose of giving colored men and women a knowledge of the English Bible; implanting in their hearts a noble ambition to go out into the dark and benighted districts of the South and give their lives for the elevation and Christianizing of the South. Last year eighty-three students attended this department. This was the largest attendance since the department was founded.

Washington stated at Memorial Hall,

Columbus, Ohio, May 24, 1900 (*The Booker T. Washington Papers*, Vol. 5: 1899-1900, University of Illinois Press, 1976, p. 543-544):

> Dr. Washington began his address after a quartet sang. He spoke of the 91 YMCA Organizations for colored youths; of the 5,000 colored men studying the Bible, and of the 640 Bible students at Tuskegee.

One of the Bible classes at Tuskegee was taught by Dr. George Washington Carver, who wrote to Booker T. Washington, on May 28, 1907:

> For your information only. Mr. B.T. Washington: About three months ago 6 or 7 persons met in my office one evening and organized a Bible class, and asked me to teach it. I consented to start them off. Their idea was to put in the 20 or 25 minutes on Sunday evenings which intervene between supper and chapel service.
>
> We began at the first of the Bible and attempted to explain the Creation story in the light of natural and revealed religion and geological truths.
>
> Maps, charts, plants, and geological specimens were used to illustrate the work. We have had an average attendance of 80 and often as high as 114. Thought these facts would help you in speaking of the religious life of the school. Very truly. G.W. Carver.

14. PRESIDENT WILLIAM MCKINLEY'S VISIT

In November of 1897, Booker T. Washington arrived at the White House and met Republican President William McKinley. He wrote:

> In a few minutes word came from Mr. McKinley that he would see me. How any man can see so many people ... and still keep himself calm, patient, and fresh for each visitor in the way that President McKinley does, I cannot understand.
>
> When I saw the President, he kindly thanked me or the work which we were doing at Tuskegee for the interests of the country. I then told him, briefly, the object of my visit. I impressed upon him the fact that a visit from the Chief Executive of the Nation would not only encourage our students and teachers but would help the entire race.

Washington wrote further:

> I went to Washington again and saw him, with a view of getting him to extend his trip to Tuskegee.
>
> On this second visit Mr. Charles W. Hare, a prominent white citizen of Tuskegee, kindly volunteered to accompany me, to reinforce my

invitation with one from the white people of Tuskegee and the vicinity ...

I saw the President ... I perceived that his heart was greatly burdened by reason of these race disturbances. Although there were many people waiting to see him, he detained me for some time, discussing the condition and prospects of the race.

He remarked several times that he was determined to show his interest and faith in the race, not merely in words, but by acts.

Washington continued:

While I was with the President, a white citizen of Atlanta, a Democrat and an ex-slaveholder, came into the room, and the President asked his opinion as to the wisdom of his going to Tuskegee.

Without hesitation the Atlanta man replied that it was the proper thing for him to do ... The President promised that he would visit our school on the 16th of December ...

When it became known that the President was going to visit our school, the white citizens of the town of Tuskegee — a mile distant from the school were as much pleased as were our students and teachers.

The white people of the town, including both men and women, began arranging to decorate the town ... I think I never realized before this how much the white people of Tuskegee and vicinity thought of our institution ... Dozens of these people came to me and said ... if there was anything they could do to help, or to relieve me personally,

I had but to intimate it and they would be only too glad to assist ... The thing that touched me almost as deeply as the visit of the President itself was the deep pride which all classes of citizens in Alabama seemed to take in our work.

In 1898, President William McKinley visited Tuskegee and described the institute as "progressive," calling Washington "one of the great leaders of his race." Washington wrote:

The morning of December 16th brought to the little city of Tuskegee such a crowd as it had never seen before.

With the President came Mrs. McKinley and all of the Cabinet officers but one; and most of them brought their wives or some members of their families ... There was also a host of newspaper correspondents.

The Alabama Legislature was in session at Montgomery at this time. This body passed a resolution to adjourn for the purpose of visiting Tuskegee ... The citizens of Tuskegee had decorated the town from the station to the school in a generous manner. In order to economize in the matter of time, we arranged to have the whole school pass in review before the President ...

Each student carried a stalk of sugarcane with some open bolls of cotton fastened to the end of it. Following the students, the work of all departments of the school passed in review, displayed on "floats" drawn by horses, mules, and oxen ...

In his address in our large, new chapel, which the students had recently completed, the President said:

"Tuskegee Normal and Industrial Institute is ideal in its conception, and has already a large and growing reputation in the country, and is not unknown abroad. I congratulate all who are associated in this undertaking for the good work which it is doing in the education of its students to lead lives of honor and usefulness, thus exalting the race for which it was established ...

"To speak of Tuskegee without paying special tribute to Booker T. Washington's genius and perseverance would be impossible. The inception of this noble enterprise was his, and he deserves high credit for it.

"His was the enthusiasm and enterprise which made its steady progress possible and established in the institution its present high standard of accomplishment. He has won a worthy reputation as one of the great leaders of his race, widely known and much respected at home and abroad as an accomplished educator, a great orator, and a true philanthropist."

Secretary of the Navy John D. Long then spoke in honor of Booker T. Washington at Tuskegee:

> I cannot make a speech today. My heart is too full—full of hope, admiration, and pride for my countrymen of both sections and both colors. I am filled with gratitude and admiration for your work, and from this time forward I shall have absolute confidence in your progress and in the solution of the problem in which you are engaged. The problem, I say, has been solved ...

Long continued:

> A picture has been presented today which should be put upon canvas with the pictures of Washington and Lincoln, and transmitted to future time and generations — a picture which the press of the country should spread broadcast over the land, a most dramatic picture, and that picture is this:
>
> "The President of the United States standing on this platform; on one side the Governor of Alabama, on the other, completing the trinity, a representative of a race only a few years ago in bondage, the colored President of the Tuskegee Normal and Industrial Institute."

Secretary of the Navy John D. Long concluded:

> God bless the President under whose majesty such a scene as that is presented to the American people. God bless the

state of Alabama, which is showing that it can deal with this problem for itself. God bless the orator, philanthropist, and disciple of the Great Master — who, if he were on earth, would be doing the same work — Booker T. Washington.

Secretary of the Navy John D. Long wrote to his wife, Agnes Pierce Long, during the Spanish-American War, October 9, 1898:

> The Tenth Regular Infantry ... is composed, with the exception of the officers, entirely of colored men. It is one of the regiments which did the very best work in the Santiago campaign, and no soldiers fought better ...
>
> They marched with an easy light step; they had the faces of their race. It was a great day for them and for the colored people who cheered them on the way ... I could not help thinking of this race a few years ago in slavery and today freemen and citizens.
>
> How barbarous seems the color discrimination, when in every walk of life they are making the same progress as the white man; when their Booker T. Washington is, perhaps, the finest orator in the country, and these troops are the best fighting soldiers of the war.

15. HARVARD HONORARY DOCTORATE & RECOGNITION

In 1896, Washington was awarded an honorary master's degree from Harvard—the first New England university to confer an honorary degree upon a black man.

Harvard President Charles W. Eliot wrote May 28, 1896:

> President Booker T. Washington,
>
> My Dear Sir,
>
> Harvard University desires to confer on you at the approaching Commencement an honorary degree; but it is our custom to confer degrees only on gentlemen who are present.
>
> Our Commencement occurs this year on June 24, and your presence would be desirable from about noon till about five o'clock in the afternoon.
>
> Would it be possible for you to be in Cambridge on that day? Believe me, with great regard,
>
> Very truly yours, Charles W. Eliot.

Harvard President Eliot spoke at Tuskegee's 25th anniversary in 1906, stating:

> By 1905, Tuskegee produced more self-made millionaires than Harvard,

Yale and Princeton combined.

Dartmouth awarded Booker T. Washington an honorary doctorate in 1901.

Washington addressed innumerable audiences and wrote numerous articles and books: *The Future of the American Negro*, 1899; *Up From Slavery*, 1901; *The Story of My Life and Work*, 1901; *Character Building*, 1902; *Working with the Hands*, 1904; *Tuskegee & Its People*, 1905; *Frederick Douglass*, 1906; *The Negro in the South*, 1907; *The Man Farthest Down: A Record of Observation and Study in Europe*, 1912.

Visitors came to Tuskegee from 16 countries, including Africa, India, China, Japan, Poland and Russia. He sent Tuskegee graduates to Liberia, West Africa, and even sent his personal envoy, Emmitt Scott, to discourage France from annexing Liberia, helping preserve Liberia's independence.

In 1899, he and his wife, Margaret, traveled to Europe, where they met many dignitaries, including being honored by an invitation to Windsor Castle in England for tea with Queen Victoria. Washington wrote in his autobiography *Up From Slavery* (1901):

> Through the kindness of Lady Aberdeen, my wife and I were enabled ... to see Queen Victoria, at Windsor Castle, where, afterward, we were all the guests of her Majesty at tea. In our party was Miss Susan B. Anthony, and I was deeply impressed with the fact that one did not often get an opportunity to see, during the same hour, two women

so remarkable in different ways as Susan B. Anthony and Queen Victoria.

He described further:

> When the Englishman takes you into his heart and friendship, he binds you there as with cords of steel, and I do not believe that there are many other friendships that are so lasting or so satisfactory. Perhaps I can illustrate this point in no better way than by relating the following incident.
>
> Mrs. Washington and I were invited to attend a reception given by the Duke and Duchess of Sutherland, at Stafford House said to be the finest house in London; I may add that I believe the Duchess of Sutherland is said to be the most beautiful woman in England.
>
> There must have been at least three hundred persons at this reception. Twice during the evening the Duchess sought us out for a conversation, and she asked me to write her when we got home, and tell her more about the work at Tuskegee. This I did.
>
> When Christmas came we were surprised and delighted to receive her photograph with her autograph on it. The correspondence has continued, and we now feel that in the Duchess of Sutherland we have one of our warmest friends.

He noted:

> In introducing me to an audience in Essex Hall, London, during my

visit to Europe, in the summer of 1899, Honorable Joseph H. Choate, the American Ambassador, said that I was one of the few Americans that had had the opportunity of choosing his own name, and in exercising the rare privilege I had very naturally chosen the best name there was in the list.

In *The Story of My Life & Work*, Booker T. Washington wrote:

> Early in August we sailed for America from Southampton, and had a very pleasant voyage on the magnificent ocean steamer *St. Louis*. On the voyage I was called upon to speak again to the passengers, and made many friends for our cause.
>
> While in Europe I received the following invitation ... May 16, 1899 ...
>
> "Dear Sir:—
>
> "We, the citizens of Charleston and West Virginia, desire to express our pride in you and the splendid career you have thus far accomplished, and ask that we be permitted to show our pride and interest in a substantial way.
>
> "Your recent visit to your old home in our midst awoke within us the keenest regret that we were not permitted to hear you and render some substantial aid to your work, before you left for Europe.
>
> "In view of the foregoing, we earnestly invite you to share the hospitality of our city upon your return

from Europe and give us the opportunity to hear you and put ourselves in touch with your work in a way that will be most gratifying to yourself, and that we may receive the inspiration of your words and presence.

"An early reply to this invitation, with an indication of the time you may reach our city will greatly oblige."

This invitation to accept a reception from the citizens of Charleston, W. Va., where I had spent my boyhood days, was a very satisfactory surprise.

When I left Charleston, and when I left Malden, which is very near Charleston, I was quite a boy, and I had not been able to spend any great length of time there since I had first left to enter the Hampton Institute.

I accepted the invitation for the Charleston reception, and when I reached Charleston was met by a committee of citizens headed by ex-Gov. W.A. MacCorkle.

The meeting in connection with this reception was held in the opera house, and was presided over by Gov. George W. Atkinson. It was very largely attended by white and colored citizens from that vicinity, a large number of whom had known me in my boyhood days.

I must refrain from giving any detailed account of all the kind and complimentary things they were kind enough to say about me at this meeting. I spent several days in Charleston, visiting the scenes of my early boyhood, and my sister in Malden, and many of the older citizens who remembered me.

After this reception in Charleston I was invited to go to Atlanta, Georgia, by the white and colored citizens, to be given a reception there. The meeting in Atlanta was presided over by the Governor of the State, and was largely attended.

Receptions by the citizens of Montgomery and New Orleans soon followed. Invitations to attend receptions in other states came to me, but I was not able to accept them all.

In the fall of 1899, a meeting was held at Huntsville, Alabama, the spirit of which has since been taken up by other Southern cities, which promises to prove of lasting benefit in settling the race problem in the South.

In October a meeting was called at Huntsville, which had for its object the discussion of all matters relating to the upbuilding of the South. It was well attended by representatives from nearly every Southern State, and was a strong body of men.

16. ADVISOR TO PRESIDENTS

In the post-Civil War Reconstruction era, blacks worked hard to advance. When Southern Democrat vigilante groups retaliated, Republican President Ulysses S. Grant outlawed those groups by signing the Klu Klux Klan Act of 1871. On October 18, 1871, he deployed U.S. troops south to combat violence against African-Americans.

Grant stated March 4, 1873:

> The effects of the late civil strife have been to free the slave and make him a citizen. Yet he is not possessed of the civil rights which citizenship should carry with it. This is wrong, and should be corrected. To this correction I stand committed.

Grant supported the 15th Amendment guaranteeing black men the right to vote. It passed in Congress over a 97 percent Democrat opposition. Grant stated in 1885:

> Four millions of human beings held as chattels have been liberated; the ballot has been given to them.

White Republicans went south to register freed blacks to vote. Democrats called them "radicals" and lynched many along with blacks.

The Republican Party splintered into rivalries during the 1876 Presidential Election. Democrats agreed to support candidate Rutherford B. Hayes if he would end Reconstruction by pulling Federal troops out of the South. Unfortunately, Hayes caved, allowing Democrat racism to continue.

The 20th President, Republican James Garfield, stated in his Inaugural Address, March 4, 1881:

> Let our people find a new meaning in the divine oracle which declares that "a little child shall lead them," for our own little children will soon control the destinies of the Republic ...
>
> Our children ... will surely bless their fathers and their fathers' God that the Union was preserved, that slavery was overthrown, and that both races were made equal before the law.

Before Garfield was assassinated, he appointed African-Americans to prominent positions: Frederick Douglass, Recorder of Deeds; Robert Brown Elliot, Special Agent to the U.S. Treasury; John M. Langston, Haitian Minister; and Blanche K. Bruce, Register to the U.S. Treasury.

In 1898, a mob of 2,000 Southern Democrats in Wilmington, North Carolina, rioted to overthrow the elected bi-racial Fusionist government, formed from Republican and Populist Party members. The mob expelled blacks and their Republican supporters, killing an estimated 300.

In the Spanish-American War, 1898, Republican President William McKinley integrated black and white soldiers and sailors. The 5,000 black soldiers, called "Buffalo Soldiers" by the Indians, were nicknamed "Immunes" in Cuba as they were considered immune to tropical diseases.

General "Black Jack" Pershing, Republican, said:

> The entire command moved forward as coolly as though the buzzing of bullets was the humming of bees ... white regiments, black regiments, regulars and Rough Riders, representing the young manhood of the North and the South, fought shoulder to shoulder, unmindful of race or color, unmindful of whether commanded by ex-Confederate or not, and mindful of only their common duty as Americans.

Tuskegee Institute recorded that from 1882-1968, there were 4,743 documented lynchings: 3,446 blacks and 1,297 whites, who were "radical" Republicans caught registering freed blacks to vote. Instead of a black versus white issue, it is a Republican versus Democrat issue.

When McKinley was assassinated, Republican Theodore Roosevelt became the 26th President. He stated in his State of the Union, December 3, 1906:

> White men are lynched, but the crime is peculiarly frequent in respect to black men ... Governor Candler, of Georgia, stated ... "I can say of a verity that I have, within the last month, saved the lives of half a dozen innocent Negroes who were pursued by the mob, and brought them to trial in a court of law in which they were acquitted" ...
>
> As Bishop Charles Galloway of Mississippi has finely said: "The mob that lynches a Negro charged with rape will in a little while lynch a white man suspected of crime. Every Christian patriot in

America needs to lift up his voice in loud and eternal protest against the mob spirit that is threatening the integrity of this Republic ...

There is but one safe rule ... that is, to treat each man, whatever his color, his creed, or his social position, with evenhanded justice ... Reward or punish the individual on his merits as an individual. Evil will surely come in the end to both races if we substitute for this ...

Every lynching represents ... a loosening of the bands of civilization ... No man can take part in the torture of a human being without having his own moral nature permanently lowered.

Every lynching means just so much moral deterioration in all the children who have any knowledge of it, and therefore just so much additional trouble for the next generation of Americans.

Theodore Roosevelt was the first President to invite an African-American, Booker T. Washington, to be an honored guest for dinner at the White House, October 16, 1901. This acknowledgment added to Booker T. Washington's status as the nation's leading black spokesman.

Democrats were furious. The newspaper, *The Memphis Scimitar*, printed:

The most damnable outrage which has ever been perpetrated by any citizen of the United States was committed yesterday by the President, when he invited a n---- to dine with him at the

White House.

It would not be worth more than a passing notice if Theodore Roosevelt had sat down to dinner in his own home with a Pullman car porter, but Roosevelt the individual and Roosevelt the President are not to be viewed in the same light.

Democrat Senator Ben Tillman of South Carolina vented:

The action of President Roosevelt in entertaining that n****r will necessitate our killing a thousand n****rs in the South before they will reach their place again.

(*Ben Tillman and the Reconstruction of White Supremacy,* 2000, Stephen Kantrowitz. Univ. of North Carolina Press, p. 259)

Booker T. Washington wrote to President Roosevelt, October 26, 1901:

I have refrained from writing you regarding the now famous dinner in which both of us ate so innocently ... I believe that a great deal is being made over the incident because of the elections which are now pending in several Southern states.

Roosevelt responded to the criticism:

The only wise and honorable and Christian thing to do is to treat each black man and each white man strictly on his merits as a man.

Following Roosevelt, the 27th President was Republican William Howard Taft. He held Booker T. Washington in esteem as advisor, remarking at Carnegie Hall, February 23, 1909 (quoted in *The Times,* February 25, 1909, p. 5):

> The race that can produce a Booker T. Washington in a century ought to feel it can do miracles in time.

Many Democrat states had black codes, or Jim Crow Laws which prohibited blacks from gun ownership or restricted their learning to read and write. One black code required blacks ride in separate, and often inferior, railroad cars. In 1892, a black man, Homer Plessy, was arrested for violating the Louisiana Separate Car Act. The Supreme Court upheld this discrimination in *Plessy v. Ferguson*, 1896, calling it "separate but equal."

The 28th President was Democrat Woodrow Wilson He considered *Plessy v. Ferguson* as "stare decisis"– settled law, and proceeded to segregate the U.S. Army, the U.S. Navy, the Postal Service, the Treasury, and other Federal offices. In 1914, a protest delegation met with Wilson led by black representative Monroe Trotter. Wilson told him:

> Segregation is not humiliating, but a benefit, and ought to be so regarded by you gentlemen. If your organization goes out and tells the colored people of the country that it is ... a benefit, they will regard it the same. The only harm that will come will be if you cause them to think it is a humiliation.

Monroe Trotter replied:

> Soon after your inauguration began, segregation was drastically introduced in the Treasury and Postal departments by your appointees.

Wilson snapped back:

> If this organization is ever to have another hearing before me it must have another spokesman. Your manner offends me ... Your tone, with its background of passion.

Wilson screened the pro Klu Klux Klan movie, *The Clansman* (1915), in the White House, which led to a revival of KKK membership.

In 1920, Warren G. Harding accepted the Republican nomination for President. He stated:

> No majority shall abridge the rights of a minority ... I believe the Negro citizens of America should be guaranteed the enjoyment of all their rights, that they have earned their full measure of citizenship bestowed, that their sacrifices in blood on the battlefields of the republic have entitled them to all of freedom and opportunity, all of sympathy and aid that the American spirit of fairness and justice demands.

When Harding became the 29th President, he asked Congress to pass an anti-lynching bill. He condemned the Democrat white supremacist mob that committed the Tulsa massacre in 1921, destroying Black Wall Street, a 35 square block area of black-owned businesses, killing 300 African-Americans and leaving 10,000 homeless.

Harding responded by giving an address at Pennsylvania's Lincoln University, known as "the Black Princeton" for being the nation's first historically black institution to grant degrees. He addressed the student body as "my fellow countrymen," stating:

> Despite the demagogues, the idea of our oneness as Americans has risen superior to every appeal to mere class and group ... And so, I wish it might be in this matter of our national problem of races ... God grant that, in the soberness, the fairness and the justice of this country, we never see another spectacle like it.

Afterwards, Harding greeted the graduates "and shook hands with each one of them." He honored the 367,000 black servicemen who fought in World War I, including Lincoln University graduate Colonel F.A. Denison, the sole black commander of a regiment in France, of the 370th U.S. Infantry "Black Devils." The university newspaper described the visit "the high-water mark in the history of the institution."

Harding addressed a crowd of 100,000 in Birmingham, Alabama, calling for equality among races, educationally, economically, and politically:

> Let the black man vote when he is fit to vote; and prohibit the white man voting when he is unfit to vote ... What I say on this I say to all America, north and south, white and black. Whether you like it or not, unless our democracy is a lie, you must recognize that equality.

Tuskegee's new Principal, Dr. Robert Russa Moton, called Harding's speech "the most important utterance on the question by a President since Lincoln." Major Adam E. Patterson, the first Black Judge Advocate of the all-Black 92nd Division in World War I, wrote in the *Voice of the People* that Harding's speech was on par with Lincoln's Gettysburg Address, "especially so since he made it where it will do the most good."

Democrats had the opposite reaction. A Democrat Congressman from Mississippi called Harding's words "a blow to the white civilization of America." Georgia's Democrat Senator Thomas Watson claimed Harding planted "fatal germs in the minds of the black race." *The Selma Times-Journal* printed:

> If the President's theory is carried to its ultimate conclusion, namely, the that black person either man or woman, should have full economic and political rights with the white man and white woman, then that means that the black can strive to become President of the United States; hold cabinet positions, and occupy the highest places of public trust in the nation ... I am against any such theory because I know it is impracticable, it is unjust, and it is destructive of the best ideals of America.

Harding's Republican Vice-President, Calvin Coolidge, traveled to Tuskegee in 1923 to meet Dr. Robert Russa Moton. When Harding died, Coolidge was the 30th President. He arranged for Moton to meet him in 1924 in the White House.

Dr. Moton went on to advise five U.S. Presidents. He commented in "The Negro of To-Day," *The Times Supplement,* July 4, 1921:

> The vast majority of Negros are members of or associated with either the Baptist Church or the several branches

of the Methodist Church ...

So strong has been their allegiance to these two denominations that Dr. Booker T. Washington used to say, with his characteristic humor, that if ever you discovered a Negro who was not either a Baptist or a Methodist, some white man had been tampering with his religion.

Coolidge remarked December 6, 1923:

Numbered among our population are some 12,000,000 colored people. Under our Constitution their rights are just as sacred as those of any other citizen. It is both a public and a private duty to protect those rights ... Congress ought to exercise all its powers of prevention and punishment against the hideous crime of lynching, of which the Negroes are by no means the sole sufferers, but for which they furnish a majority of the victims ...

A considerable sum is appropriated to give the Negroes vocational training in agriculture ... About half a million dollars is recommended for medical courses at Howard University to help contribute to the education of 500 colored doctors needed each year.

Coolidge stated June 6, 1924, at Howard University's commencement, Washington, D.C.:

Colored people have repeatedly proved their devotion to the high ideals of our country. They gave their services in the war with the same patriotism and readiness that other citizens did. The records of the selective draft show that somewhat more than 2,250,000 colored men were registered ... Far from seeking to avoid participation in the national defense, they showed that they wished to enlist before the selective service act was put into operation.

Coolidge wrote to Charles F. Gardner, Fort Hamilton, New York, August 9, 1924:

> During the war 500,000 colored men and boys were called up under the draft, not one of whom sought to evade it. They took their places wherever assigned in defense of the nation of which they are just as truly citizens as are any others. The suggestion of denying any measure of their full political rights ... is one which ... could not possibly be permitted by one who feels a responsibility for living up to the traditions and maintaining the principles of the Republican Party.
>
> Our Constitution guarantees equal rights to all our citizens, without discrimination on account of race or color ... A colored man is precisely as much entitled to submit his candidacy in a party primary as is any other citizen.

Coolidge stated December 3, 1924:

> Colored people ... should be cheerfully accorded their full constitutional rights, that they should be protected ... especially from the crime of lynching and that they should receive every encouragement to become full partakers in all the blessings of our

common American citizenship.

Republican Herbert Hoover, the 31st President, gave a radio address from the White House, April 14, 1931:

> I consider it a great privilege to take even a small part in this celebration of the 50th anniversary of Tuskegee Institute. Established half a century ago by Booker T. Washington ... it has grown into a great national educational institution devoted to the development of the Negro race and ... its advancement. It is now over 60 years since the Negro was released from slavery and given the status of a citizen in our country whose wealth and general prosperity his labor has helped create.
>
> The progress of the race within this period has surpassed the most sanguine hopes of the most ardent advocates. No group of people in history ever started from a more complete economic and cultural destitution ... Within that period the race has multiplied its wealth more than 130 times, has reduced its illiteracy from 95 percent to 20 percent, and reduced its death rate by one-half. It has risen to the ownership of more than 750,000 homes, has accumulated property to the value of billions, has developed a far-reaching internal network of social, religious, and economic organizations for the continued advancement of its people, has produced leadership in all walks of life that for faith, courage, devotion, and patriotic loyalty ...
>
> The greatest single factor in the progress of the Negro race has been the schools, private and public, established

and conducted by high minded, self-sacrificing men and women of both races ...

Public and private schools, particularly under the leadership of Tuskegee ... have been the most effective agents in solving the problems created by the admission to citizenship of 4 million ex-slaves without preparation for their new responsibilities. That such a revolution in the social order did not produce a more serious upheaval in our national existence has been due to the constructive influence exerted by these educational institutions ...

The Nation owes a debt of gratitude to the wisdom and constructive vision of Booker T. Washington ... His conception of education based fundamentally upon vocational and moral training has been worthily continued by his able successor, Dr. R.R. Moton.

Booker T. Washington's nephew, Roscoe Conkling Simmons (1881–1951), was a Republican Party leader and journalist, being the first African-American columnist hired by the *Chicago Tribune*.

Democrat Senate Majority Leader Robert Byrd, the longest serving U.S. Senator, stated: "You had to be in the Klan to advance in the Democrat Party."

On June 29, 2021, Congress passed a bill removing from the Capitol statues of pro-slavery politicians. Minority Leader Kevin McCarthy noted:

All of the statues being removed by this bill are statues of Democrats.

17. RISING ABOVE CRITICS

Booker T. Washington had to walk a fine line between Southern Democrat racists and Northern activists. Those in the North had little comprehension of dangers faced daily by blacks in the South surrounded by vigilante groups who retaliated if blacks rose too fast in social position.

One Northern activist was W.E.B. Du Bois in Boston, who addressed racial injustices from an intellectual perspective. Several churches paid his tuition to attend Fisk University, after which he graduated from the elite Harvard University.

Du Bois studied in Germany, describing it as the "great socialistic state of the day." Appropriating Washington's idea of the Negro Business League, Du Bois helped found the NAACP in 1909. Visiting Germany again in 1936, the *Staatszeitung und Herold* newspaper reported Du Bois praising the National Socialist Workers Party's handling of the economy. Nazis went on to kill millions of Jews and other minorities.

In 1926, Du Bois made his first visit to the Union of Soviet Socialist Republics, just nine years after the Bolshevik Revolution. Enamored with socialism, he visited again in 1936, 1949 and 1959. Soviet policies in Russia resulted in the deaths of an estimated 40 to 60 million.

Du Bois was attracted to Marx's atheism. He

criticized churches and refused to lead public prayers, writing in his autobiography:

> When I became head of a department at Atlanta (University), the engagement was held up because again I balked at leading in prayer ... I flatly refused again to join any church or sign any church creed ... I think the greatest gift of the Soviet Union to modern civilization was the dethronement of the clergy and the refusal to let religion be taught in the public schools.

Du Bois' views gradually gained ascendancy in academia and even influenced those who wrote biographies critical of Washington. Du Bois had a falling out with the vocal segregationist Marcus Garvey, whom Du Bois labeled as "dangerous."

In 1958, Du Bois visited East Germany where a communist university gave him an honorary doctorate. In 1959, Du Bois visited Mao Zedung in the People's Republic of China. Deaths from China's communist policies are estimated from 60 to 80 million. In 1961, Du Bois joined the U.S. Communist Party, writing in his application:

> On this first day of October 1961, I am applying for admission to membership in the Communist Party of the United States ...
>
> At the University of Berlin ... I attended meetings of the Socialist Party and considered myself a Socialist. On my return to America ... I came to New York as an official of the new NAACP ... It had a strong socialist element in its leadership ...

> I ... advised Negroes to vote for Wilson ... For the next twenty years ... I praised the racial attitudes of the Communists ...
>
> I began the study Karl Marx and the Communists; I read *Das Kapital* and other Communist literature; I hailed the Russian Revolution of 1917 ...
>
> In 1926, I began a new effort; I visited the Communist lands. I went to the Soviet Union in 1926, 1936, 1949 and 1959 ... I visited East Germany, Czechoslovakia and Poland. I spent ten weeks in China, traveling all over the land ... I was early convinced that socialism was an excellent way of life, but I thought it might be reached by various methods ...
>
> Today I have reached my conclusion ... The path of the American Communist Party is clear ... It will call for: public ownership of natural resources and of all capital ... public control of transportation and communications ... limitation of personal income ... social medicine ... Free education for all ... No dogmatic religion - W.E.B. Du Bois."

A similar statement was made by Roger Baldwin, a World War I draft dodger who founded the American Civil Liberties Union (ACLU). Baldwin wrote in his Harvard College Class Thirtieth Anniversary Yearbook, 1935:

> I am for socialism, disarmament ... I seek social ownership of property, the abolition of the propertied class,

and sole control of those who produce wealth. Communism is the goal.

Baldwin was an ally of Planned Parenthood founder Margaret Sanger, whom he defended in St. Louis in 1912. Sanger addressed a Klu Klux Klan rally in Silver Lake, New Jersey. She began the "Negro Project" in 1939 to reduce the African-American population, writing:

> We do not want word to go out that we want to exterminate the Negro population, and the minister is the man who can straighten out that idea if it ever occurs to any of their more rebellious members.

Booker T. Washington had warned that activist views could be co-opted into stirring up racial tension for political purposes, a tactic employed by communist agitators called "critical race theory." In *My Larger Education–Being Chapters of My Experience*, 1911, Washington included a chapter "The Intellectuals and the Boston Mob":

> There is another class of colored people who make a business of keeping the troubles, the wrongs, and the hardships of the Negro race before the public.
>
> Having learned that they are able to make a living out of their troubles, they have grown into the settled habit of advertising their wrongs – partly because they want sympathy and partly because it pays ...
>
> Some of these people do not want the Negro to lose his grievances, because they do not want to lose their jobs ...

> I am afraid that there is a certain class of race problem solvers who do not want the patient to get well, because as long as the disease holds out they have not only an easy means of making a living, but also an easy medium through which to make themselves prominent before the public ...
>
> My experience is that people who call themselves "The Intellectuals" understand theories, but they do not understand things. I have long been convinced that, if these men could have gone into the South and taken up and become interested in some practical work which would have brought them in touch with people and things, the whole world would have looked very different to them.
>
> Bad as conditions might have seemed at first, when they saw that actual progress was being made, they would have taken a more hopeful view of the situation.

Washington added:

> A whining crying race may be pitied but seldom respected.

A black journalist who joined the Communist Party USA in 1943 was Frank Marshall Davis. *Investor's Business Daily* reported August 5, 2008:

> Davis was a member of the Moscow-controlled Communist Party USA, according to the 1953 report of the Commission of Subversive Activities of the Territory of Hawaii. While in Hawaii, Frank Marshall Davis wrote a

weekly column, "Frank-ly Speaking," for the labor union paper *Honolulu Record*, headed by the vocal communist, Harry Bridges.

In 1956, Davis was called to testify before the Senate Internal Security Subcommittee, In the article "Frank Marshall Davis: A Forgotten Voice" (2002), Kathryn Takara, a former University of Hawaii professor, quoted Davis as saying: "From now on I knew I would be described as a Communist." Davis later mentored a future U.S. President.

Manning Johnson was another black man who became disillusioned and joined the Communist Party. He even ran for Congress in New York on the Communist Party ticket. After ten years, he realized communists had no real interest in helping his people, but only using them for their political ends. Johnson testified in 1947 before Congress on the subversive plots to infiltrate universities, churches, entertainment, media, and business by deep-state communist operatives.

In 1958, Johnson wrote an exposé titled *Color, Communism and Common Sense,* with a foreword by Archibald Roosevelt, son of Theodore Roosevelt, who was a decorated U.S. military commander. Not long after publishing his expose' Johnson was suspiciously involved in two automobile accidents, the second of which killed him in 1959. He had stated:

> To me, the end of capitalism would mark the beginning of ... plenty, peace, prosperity and universal comradeship. All racial and class differences and

conflicts would end forever after the liquidation of the capitalists, their government and their supporters ...

Being an idealist, I was sold this "bill of goods" ... Like other Negroes, I experienced and saw many injustices and inequities around me based upon color, not ability.

I was told that "the decadent capitalist system is responsible," that "mass pressure" could force concessions but "that just prolongs the life of capitalism"; that I must unite and work with all those who ... agree that capitalism must go.

Little did I realize until I was deeply enmeshed in the red conspiracy, that ... grievances are exploited to transform idealism into a cold and ruthless weapon against the capitalist system – that this is the end toward which all the communist efforts among Negroes are directed ...

I saw communism in all its naked cruelty, ruthlessness and utter contempt of Christian attributes and passions. And, too, I saw the low value placed upon human life, the total lack of respect for the dignity of man.

Johnson continued:

After two years of practical training in organizing street demonstrations, inciting mob violence, how to fight the police and how to politically 'throw a brick and hide' ... I was given an ... intensive course in the theory and practice of red political warfare ... that changed me from a novice into a dedicated red – a professional revolutionist.

He explained further:

> I began to realize the full implications of how the Negro is used as a political dupe by the Kremlin hierarchy ...
>
> White leftists descended on Negro communities like locusts, posing as "friends" come to help 'liberate' their black brothers ... Everything was inter-racial, an inter-racialism artificially created, cleverly devised as a camouflage of the red plot to use the Negro ... beating the racial drums ... even if the Negro masses are left prostrate and bleeding — expendables in the mad scramble for power.

Malcolm X, before his assassination in 1963, said:

> The white liberal differs from the white conservative ... Both want power, but the white liberal ... has perfected the art of posing as the Negro's friend and benefactor ... to use the Negro as a pawn or a weapon in this political football game that is constantly raging between the white liberal and the white conservative ... and the white liberals control this ball.

Saul Alinsky, in his book *Rules for Radicals* (1971), gave an acknowledgment to Lucifer then went on to explain divide and conquer tactics:

> The first step in community organization is community disorganization ... Disruption of the present organization is the first step ... The organizer must first rub raw the resentments of the people of

the community; fan the latent hostilities of many of the people to the point of overt expression ... Search out controversy and issues, rather than avoid them, for unless there is controversy, people are not concerned enough to act ... The organizer's first job is to create the issues or problems ... An organizer must stir up dissatisfaction and discontent ... The organizer ... polarizes the issue ... helps to lead his forces into conflict ... The real arena is corrupt and bloody ... In war the end justifies almost any means.

Soviet dictator Joseph Stalin had stated:

> Crisis alone permitted the authorities to demand – and obtain – total submission and all necessary sacrifices from its citizens.

Franklin Roosevelt warned January 3, 1940:

> Doctrines that set group against group, faith against faith, race against race, class against class, fanning the fires of hatred in men too despondent, too desperate to think for themselves, were used as rabble-rousing slogans on which dictators could ride to power. And once in power they could saddle their tyrannies on whole nations.

Roosevelt exposed the election tactic of "race-baiting" in a campaign address. November 1, 1940:

> Those forces ... oppose Christianity because it preaches democracy ... We are a nation of many nationalities, many races, many religions – bound together by ... the unity of freedom and equality.

> Whoever seeks to set one nationality against another, seeks to degrade all nationalities. Whoever seeks to set one race against another seeks to enslave all races ... So-called racial voting blocs are the creation of designing politicians who profess to be able to deliver them on Election Day.

Roosevelt identified tactics, December 29, 1940:

> Their secret emissaries ... seek to stir up ... dissension to cause internal strife. They try to turn capital against labor ... They try to reawaken long slumbering racial and religious enmities ... These trouble-breeders have but one purpose. It is to divide our people into hostile groups and to destroy our unity.

Lincoln stated June 18, 1858: "A house divided against itself, cannot stand." Jesus warned in Mark 3:24: "If a kingdom be divided against itself, that kingdom cannot stand."

Franklin Roosevelt stated January 2, 1942:

> Remember the NAZI technique: Pit race against race, religion against religion, prejudice against prejudice. Divide and conquer!

A similar observation was made by NBA player Charles Barkley, CBS Sports panel, April 3, 2021:

> Man, I think most white people and black people are great people. I really believe that in my heart, but I think our system is set up where our politicians, whether they are Republicans or Democrats, are designed to make us

not like each other so they can keep their grasp of money and power. They divide and conquer ...

We're so stupid following our politicians ... Their only job is, "Hey ... let's make the whites and blacks not like each other, let's make rich people and poor people not like each other, let's scramble the middle class." I truly believe that in my heart.

Manning Johnson wrote:

We must try to bring America back to sanity. And let us pray and work, that the misunderstanding, the bitterness, the hate, and the frustration and the tension that exists may disappear and that the Spirit of God, the Spirit of Truth, the Spirit of Charity may prevail again amongst our people.

Intimidation tactics used to suppress black voters in the Democrat South became a political liability once television reporting put a spotlight on it. After Kennedy's assassination in 1963, Democrat President Lyndon B. Johnson began to implement *the big switch* from intimidation to entitlement as a means of manipulating minority voters – the Great Society Welfare State.

According to Ronald Kessler's *Inside The White House* (1996), Lyndon Johnson, who had a reputation for crude talk, explained his War on Poverty to two Democrat governors aboard Air Force One, saying: "I'll have those n****rs voting Democratic for the next 200 years."

African-American economist Walter E.

Williams, a Distinguished Professor of Economics at George Mason University, wrote in "The Welfare State's Legacy" (9/20/17):

> In 1960, just 22 percent of black children were raised in single-parent families. Fifty years later, more than 70 percent of black children were raised in single-parent families. Here's my question: Was the increase in single-parent black families after 1960 a legacy of slavery, or might it be a legacy of the welfare state ushered in by the War on Poverty?

African-American Republican Rep. J.C. Watts, Jr., stated February 5, 1997:

> For the past 30 years our nation's spent $5 trillion trying to erase poverty, and the result ... is that we didn't get rid of it ... We spread it. We destroyed the self-esteem of millions of people, grinding them down in a welfare system that penalizes moms for wanting to marry the father of their children, and penalizes moms for wanting to save money. Friends, that's not right

18. MARTIN LUTHER KING, JR.

A leader who followed in the footsteps of Booker T. Washington to be the nation's leading black spokesman was Martin Luther King, Jr.

As a youth, King attended Booker T. Washington High School in Atlanta, 1942-44. In 1944, he attended Morehouse College, founded in Atlanta after the Civil War by Baptist minister Rev. William Jefferson White and named for Rev. Lyman Morehouse, Secretary of the American Baptist Mission Board,

After seminary, King was pastor of Atlanta's Ebenezer Baptist Church. He rose to prominence as head of the Southern Christian Leadership Conference and was awarded the Nobel Prize in 1964. Tragically, he was assassinated in 1968.

Rev. King, along with Archbishop Desmond Tutu, had been influenced by German Confessing Church leader Dietrich Bonhoeffer, who resisted Hitler's totalitarian socialism. King was also influenced by Mahatma Gandhi's non-violent example of resisting Britain's control of India.

On April 16, 1963, Rev. King warned:
> I stand in the middle of two opposing forces in the Negro community. One is a force of complacency ... The other force is one of bitterness and hatred, and it comes perilously close to advocating violence. It is expressed

in the various black nationalist groups that are springing up across the nation, the largest and best known being Elijah Muhammad's Muslim movement.

Nourished by the Negro's frustration over the continued existence of racial discrimination, this movement is made up of people who have lost faith in America, who have absolutely repudiated Christianity, and who have concluded that the white man is an incorrigible "devil" ...

I have tried to stand between these two forces, saying that we need emulate neither the "do-nothingism" of the complacent nor the hatred of the black nationalist. For there is the more excellent way of love and non-violent protest.

I am grateful to God that, through the influence of the Negro church, the way of nonviolence became an integral part of our struggle ...

If our white brothers dismiss ... those of us who employ nonviolent direct action ... millions of Negroes will, out of frustration and despair, seek solace and security in black nationalist ideologies – a development that would inevitably lead to a frightening racial nightmare ...

One day the South will know that when these disinherited children of God sat down at lunch counters they were in reality standing up for what is best in the American dream and for the most sacred values in our Judeo-Christian heritage.

Rev. Martin Luther King, Jr., stated at the Civil Rights March in Washington, D.C., August 28, 1963:

> Now is the time to open the doors of opportunity to all of God's children. Now is the time to lift our nation from the quicksands of racial injustice to the solid rock of brotherhood ...
>
> But there is something that I must say to my people who stand on the warm threshold which leads into the palace of justice.
>
> In the process of gaining our rightful place we must not be guilty of wrongful deeds. Let us not seek to satisfy our thirst for freedom by drinking from the cup of bitterness and hatred. We must forever conduct our struggle on the high plane of dignity and discipline. We must not allow our creative protest to degenerate into physical violence ...
>
> New militancy which has engulfed the Negro community must not lead us to a distrust of all white people, for many of our white brothers, as evidenced by their presence here today, have come to realize that their destiny is tied up with our destiny and their freedom is inextricably bound to our freedom ... We cannot walk alone.

King continued:

> I still have a dream. It is a dream deeply rooted in the American dream.
>
> I have a dream that one day this nation will rise up and live out the true meaning of its creed: "We hold these

> truths to be self-evident; that all men are created equal."
>
> I have a dream that one day on the red hills of Georgia the sons of former slaves and the sons of former slave owners will be able to sit down together at the table of brotherhood ...
>
> I have a dream that my four little children will one day live in a nation where they will not be judged by the color of their skin but by the content of their character.

Rev. King then referenced Alabama's Democrat Governor George Wallace, who blocked the entrance to the University of Alabama in 1963, crying "Segregation now, segregation tomorrow, segregation forever." King continued his speech:

> I have a dream that one day down in Alabama, with its vicious racists, with its governor having his lips dripping with the words of interposition and nullification, that one day right down in Alabama little black boys and black girls will be able to join hands with little white boys and white girls as sisters and brothers.

King continued by quoting the Prophet Isaiah:

> I have a dream that one day every valley shall be exalted, every hill and mountain shall be made low, the rough places will be made plain, and the crooked places will be made straight, and the glory of the Lord shall be revealed, and all flesh shall see it together ...
>
> With this faith we will be able to

transform the jangling discords of our nation into a beautiful symphony of brotherhood. With this faith we will be able to work together, to pray together, to struggle together, to go to jail together, to stand up for freedom together, knowing that we will be free one day.

This will be the day when all of God's children will be able to sing with new meaning, "My country 'tis of thee, sweet land of liberty, of thee I sing. Land where my fathers died, land of the Pilgrims' pride, from every mountainside, let freedom ring" ...

And when this happens, and when we allow freedom to ring, when we let it ring from every village and every hamlet, from every state and every city, we will be able to speed up that day when all of God's children, black men and white men, Jews and gentiles, Protestants and Catholics, will be able to join hands and sing in the words of the old Negro spiritual,

"Free at last! Free at last! Thank God Almighty, we are free at last!"

Billy Graham described having Rev. Martin Luther King, Jr., at his 1957 New York City revival:

One night civil rights leader Dr. Martin Luther King, Jr., whom I was pleased to count a friend, gave an eloquent opening prayer at the service; he also came at my invitation to one of our team retreats during the crusade to help us understand the racial situation in America more fully.

Martin Luther King, Jr., wrote:

> Had it not been for the ministry of my good friend Dr. Billy Graham, my work in the Civil Rights Movement would not have been as successful as it has been.

Billy Graham stated:

> Jesus was not a white man; He was not a black man. He came from that part of the world that touches Africa and Asia and Europe. Christianity is not a white man's religion, and don't let anybody ever tell you that it's white or black. Christ belongs to all people; He belongs to the whole world.

Graham added:

> My study of the Bible, leading me eventually to the conclusion that not only was racial inequality wrong but Christians especially should demonstrate love toward all peoples.

Franklin Roosevelt had stated in a radio address, January 30, 1940:

> The answer to class hatred, race hatred, religious hatred ... is the free expression of the love of our fellow men.

FDR prayed on Flag Day, June 14, 1942:

> Grant us victory over the tyrants who would enslave all free men ... We can make ... a planet ... undivided by senseless distinctions of race.

Billy Graham gave the invocation at President Clinton's Inauguration, January 20, 1997:

Oh, Lord, help us to be reconciled first to you and secondly to each other. May Dr. Martin Luther King's dream finally come true for all of us. Help us to learn our courtesy to our fellow countrymen, that comes from the one who taught us that "whatever you want me to do to you, do also to them."

President Ronald Reagan addressed the United Negro College Fund, October 11, 1984

Education has always had a special place in the hearts of black Americans. Great figures like Frederick Douglass and Booker T. Washington grew up at a time when, in many parts of the country, it was actually against the law to teach black children to read and write. Yet, they overcame these injustices to become among the greatest educators our nation has ever seen.

In our own time, no less a figure than Dr. Martin Luther King, Jr., stressed the importance to black Americans of good education. Dr. King said, "We must forever conduct our struggle on the high plane of dignity and discipline" ...

Just a few decades ago, almost one American in ten lived a life that was separate and unequal because of the color of their skin—excluded from public life and from many of the professions. And throughout those hard years, millions of black Americans saw education as a shining hope for advancement. And it was the colleges you worked so hard to sustain—Tuskegee, Spelman, Fisk, and so many others—that turned that burning hope into a blazing reality.

I remember how, during the war, I narrated a film—I was in the Air Force myself—about black pilots being trained at Tuskegee Institute. They were brave young men. And one of them would go on to become a great general, a great patriot, and a national hero—Chappie James. I'll never forget how impressed I was by their esteem for Tuskegee and by their deep love of learning.

In 1958, Manning Johnson quoted Longfellow's *Psalm of Life* in referring to Washington and Carver:

> Great Negro Americans, such as Booker T. Washington and George Washington Carver, should serve both as an inspiration and a reminder to the present and successive generations of Negro Americans that they too "... can make their lives sublime and in departing leave behind them footprints in the sands of time."
>
> The great surge of progress of the Negro since slavery can be largely traced to the work and efforts of these two men ...
>
> Theirs was a deep and abiding pride of race, a firm belief in the ability of their benighted people to rise above their past and eventually stand on an equal plane with all other races. Moreover, equality was to them, not just a catchword ... but a living thing to be achieved only by demonstrated ability.

19. DEATH AND LEGACY

Booker T. Washington was tireless in his efforts on behalf of the black race. In March of 1915, he sponsored National Negro Health Week to address the issues of sanitation, hygiene, and disease prevention among the poor.

Later that year, at the age of 59, he died, November 14, 1915, possibly due to kidney or heart failure. He left to Tuskegee a $2,000,000 endowment, equivalent to $55,000,000 today.

In 1922, the Booker T. Washington Monument, "Lifting the Veil," was dedicated at the center of Tuskegee University, with the inscription:

> He lifted the veil of ignorance from his people and pointed the way to progress through education and industry.

Many places and items were named for him, including: a bridge, a mountain, a ship, an airplane, a college, parks, buildings elementary schools, middle schools, and high schools.

In 1934, Tuskegee President Robert Russa Moton promoted two African-American aviators to fly across the country. Their plane was renamed *Booker T. Washington*. In 1942, a WWII liberty ship was named in his honor, the first major oceangoing vessel named for an African-American. He was the first African-American to have his image on a U.S. postage stamp, 1940.

In 1945, Washington was the first African American elected to the Hall of Fame. In 1946, the first U.S. Coin featuring an African American had his image with the inscription "From slave cabin to Hall of Fame." In 1951, a commemorative half dollar featured both him and George W. Carver.

Industrialist Andrew Carnegie stated in an address at the Philosophical Institution of Edinburgh, October 16, 1907:

> Booker Washington is the combined Moses and Joshua of his people. Not only has he led them to the promised land, but still lives to teach them by example and precept how properly to enjoy it.

Upon receiving news of Washington's death, Carnegie expressed:

> I mourn with you today as one who shares your sorrow. America has lost one of her best and greatest citizens. History is to tell of two Washingtons. One the leader of his country and the other the leader of his race.

Theodore Roosevelt wrote in the "Preface" of Emmett J. Scott and Lyman Beecher Stowe's *Booker T. Washington: Builder of a Civilization* (1916)

> It is not hyperbole to say that Booker T. Washington was a great American. For twenty years before his death he had been the most useful, as well as the most distinguished, member of his race in the world, and one of the most useful, as well as one of the most distinguished, of American citizens of any race.

20. FINAL THOUGHTS

Picture yourself climbing up a tree-filled mountain side. With each step you leave behind an obstacle that had been blocking your vision. The trees that had been obscuring your view all but disappear as you approach the rocky summit. The air is thin and you are winded, but you press on.

Reaching the summit, your vision is no longer restricted. You can see in every direction. You look down the mountain to see the outline of your trail. Your eyes follow the trail way down to the base, and you see others preparing to embark on their own climb. You could guide them step by step, if only they could hear you.

Rarely does one ascend so high in intellect, emotional maturity, and uncompromising morality that they are able to see a path from poverty to success. Rarer still does one extract wisdom from the pinnacle, and package it to be shared with others.

Booker T. Washington not only climbed a mountain of challenges but shared his wisdom with those on the same path. Booker was able to access these moments of clarity so frequently that his words carry weight long after his passing.

The wisdom of Booker can be described as "timeless" — knowledge so true that it grows more potent and helpful with each passing year.

In the present divided world, the timeless wisdom of Booker T. Washington is a refreshing and inspiring blessing.

Booker was no stranger to adversity and suffering. From early on, his experience was one of hard work, coupled with tragedy. He endured the toughest of criticisms, all without ever considering himself a victim. Instead, he leaned into this adversity and allowed it to fuel his revolutionary perspective and undeniably accomplished life.

Booker ascended in wealth, status, and influence while seeking to bless others. By maintaining his agency and morality, he built a legacy.

Booker rose from slavery and poverty to become the head of Tuskegee University. He dined with presidents and set precedents. He uplifted his oppressed brothers and sister, while working to bring all people together.

Booker T. Washington proved himself the caliber of man worthy of admiration for generations. We hope his words have refreshed and inspired you as you climb your mountain.

Lastly and most importantly, Booker obtained his strength and courage by understanding that he, like you, is made in the image of God and accountable only to God. His faith gave him the strength not only to persevere to the mountain top but blaze a trail for others to follow.

The Strength and Genius of Booker T. Washington

www.ingramcontent.com/pod-product-compliance
Ingram Content Group UK Ltd.
Pitfield, Milton Keynes, MK11 3LW, UK
UKHW021303180426
11947UKWH00015B/985